IMAGES OF WAR

Essex Class Aircraft Carriers, 1943–1991

IMAGES OF WAR
Essex Class Aircraft Carriers, 1943–1991
RARE PHOTOGRAPHS FROM NAVAL ARCHIVES

LEO MARRIOTT

PEN & SWORD
MARITIME

First published in Great Britain in 2020 by
Pen & Sword Maritime
an imprint of
Pen & Sword Books Ltd
Yorkshire – Philadelphia

Copyright © Leo Marriott, 2020

ISBN 978 1 52677 214 5

The right of Leo Marriott to be identified as Author of this work has been asserted by him in accordance with the Copyright, Designs and Patents Act 1988.

A CIP catalogue record for this book is available from the British Library

All rights reserved. No part of this book may be reproduced or transmitted in any form or by any means, electronic or mechanical including photocopying, recording or by any information storage and retrieval system, without permission from the Publisher in writing.

Typeset in 12/14.5 Gill Sans by
Aura Technology and Software Services, India

Printed and bound by CPI UK

Pen & Sword Books Ltd incorporates the imprints of Pen & Sword
Archaeology, Atlas, Aviation, Battleground, Discovery, Family History, History, Maritime, Military, Naval, Politics, Social History, Transport, True Crime, Claymore Press, Frontline Books, Praetorian Press, Seaforth Publishing and White Owl

For a complete list of Pen & Sword titles please contact
47 Church Street, Barnsley, South Yorkshire, S70 2AS, England
E-mail: enquiries@pen-and-sword.co.uk
Website: www.pen-and-sword.co.uk

Or

PEN AND SWORD BOOKS
1950 Lawrence Rd, Havertown, PA 19083, USA
E-mail: Uspen-and-sword@casematepublishers.com
Website: www.penandswordbooks.com

Contents

Abbreviations .... **vii**

Introduction .... **ix**

Chapter One
US Navy Aircraft Carrier Development, 1919–41 .... **1**

Chapter Two
Essex Class Enter Service **20**

Chapter Three
Across the Pacific **37**

Chapter Four
Aboard the Essex Class **49**

Chapter Five
Through Kamikaze to Victory **68**

Chapter Six
The Post-war Era and Korea **89**

Chapter Seven
Steam and Mirrors **117**

Chapter Eight
Submarines, Spacecraft and Vietnam **137**

Chapter Nine
Postscript **155**

Photo Credits **163**

Bibliography **164**

In August 1944 USS *Bennington* (CV-20) was the eleventh Essex class carrier to enter service. (NARA)

Abbreviations

AA	Anti-Aircraft
AAA	Automatic Anti-Aircraft
AEW	Airborne Early Warning
ASW	Anti-Submarine Warfare
C-in-C	Commander-in-Chief
CAG or CVG	Carrier Air Group
DP	Dual Purpose gun
EW	Electronic Warfare
ECM	Electronic Countermeasures
HMS	His Majesty's Ship
NAS	Naval Air Station
RAF	Royal Air Force
RAS	Replenishment at Sea
RN	Royal Navy
TG	Task Group
US	United States
USAAF	US Army Air Force
USMC	United States Marine Corps
USN	United States Navy
USS	United States Ship
VA	US Navy Attack Squadron
VB	US Navy Dive Bomber Squadron
VF	US Navy Fighter Squadron
VFN	US Navy Night Fighter Squadron
VT	US Navy Torpedo Bomber Squadron
VX	US Navy Experimental Squadron

Note on US Navy Ship Designations

US Navy ships were (and still are) identified by a combination of letters indicating the ship's role followed by a sequential number for that type of ship. Role letters included

BB (Battleship), CA and CL (Heavy and Light Cruisers) and DD (Destroyer). The first US aircraft carrier (USS *Langley*) was designated CV-1, the letters CV standing for Carrier – Heavier than Air (to distinguish it from ships designed to support airship operations) and subsequent carriers received sequential numbers. The Essex class carriers were numbered from CV-9 onwards but after the Second World War the prefix was changed in some cases to reflect specialised roles including CVS (anti-submarine carrier) and CVA (attack carrier). Designations for other classes of aircraft carrier included CVL (Light Aircraft Carrier) and CVE (Escort Carrier).

Introduction

When the Imperial Japanese Navy attacked Pearl Harbor on 7 December 1941 the US Navy possessed seven aircraft carriers, none of which were present that morning and therefore all escaped any damage or loss. Over the next twelve months the nature of naval warfare was revolutionised by carrier forces engaging each other over distances far greater than any gun could reach. After the indecisive Battle of the Coral Sea in April 1942 (in which the US carrier *Lexington* was lost) the pace of Japanese advances was effectively halted by the US victory in the Battle of Midway (June 1942) in which four enemy carriers were sunk, although the USS *Yorktown* was also sunk. An attempt by Japanese forces to establish an airfield on Guadalcanal in the Solomon Islands in August 1942 was the trigger for a

Completed in December 1942, USS *Essex* (CV-9) was the first of no less than twenty-four similar vessels. (NARA)

hard-fought and bloody campaign, both on the island and at sea. In the course of two more carrier engagements (Eastern Solomons and Santa Cruz), the USS *Hornet* was sunk and the USS *Enterprise* seriously damaged. In the same period the USS *Wasp* was torpedoed and sunk by a Japanese submarine so that by the end of 1942 the US Navy had only a single carrier (USS *Saratoga*) available for operations in the Pacific; the only other serviceable carrier, USS *Ranger*, was deployed in the east Atlantic in support of the Allied landings in North Africa (Operation Torch).

At that stage the Japanese advances in the Pacific had been halted but any question of an Allied advance and eventual victory over Japan seemed a very distant and complex objective. How this was to be achieved generated much debate and fierce arguments between the US Navy and Army. The latter, under the C-in-C South Pacific (COMSOPAC) General Douglas MacArthur, advocated an island-hopping campaign through the Solomons with the eventual objective of liberating the Philippines which could then be used as a springboard for the final assault on Japan. On the other hand, the US Navy regarded the Solomons campaign as a sideshow and favoured

The after flight deck of USS *Lexington* (CV-16) in 1943 with Douglas SBD dive bombers ranged aft. (NARA)

strong naval task forces spearheading a campaign across the Central Pacific, initially to capture the Marinas from where USAAF bombers could reach Japan, and then to mount an assault on the islands of the Japanese homeland.

In the event, both strategies were adopted, partly because in late 1942 and early 1943 the US Navy did not possess the necessary warships to conduct the Central Pacific strategy. The core of any of the task forces would be aircraft carriers and their squadrons of aircraft and these were needed in substantial numbers before any major operations could be mounted. Fortunately, even by the time of Pearl Harbor, the design of a new large carrier which would become the Essex class had been finalised, and the first five hulls had already been laid down. These ships and their subsequent sisters would form the backbone of the Pacific task forces from mid-1943 onwards and by the end of the war in August 1945 no less than seventeen had been commissioned. A further seven were subsequently completed and Essex class carriers later served in both the Korean and Vietnam wars. Their story is told in the following pages.

USS *Shangri-La* (CV-38), one of many Essex class modernised in the 1950s so that they could operate the latest jets. (NARA)

Essex Class Aircraft Carriers – Construction Programme

Ship	Builder	Laid Down	Launched	Commissioned
Essex (CV-9)	Newport News	28 Apr. 1941	31 Jul. 1942	31. Dec 1942
Yorktown (CV-10)	Newport News	1 Dec. 1941	21 Jan. 1943	15 Apr. 1943
Intrepid (CV-11)	Newport News	1 Dec. 1941	26 Apr. 1943	16 Aug. 1943
Hornet (CV-12)	Newport News	3 Aug. 1942	30 Aug. 1943	29 Nov. 1943
Franklin (CV-13)	Newport News	7 Dec. 1942	14 Oct. 1943	31 Jan. 1944
Ticonderoga (CV-14)	Newport News	1 Feb. 1943	7 Feb. 1944	8 May 1944
Randolph (CV-15)	Newport News	10 May 1943	29 Jun. 1944	9 Oct. 1944
Lexington (CV-16)	Bethlehem	15 Sep. 1941	26 Sep. 1942	17 Feb. 1943
Bunker Hill (CV-17)	Bethlehem	15 Sep. 1941	7 Dec. 1942	25 May 1943
Wasp (CV-18)	Bethlehem	18 Mar. 1942	17 Aug. 1943	24 Nov. 1943
Hancock (CV-19)	Bethlehem	26 Jan. 1943	24 Jan. 1944	15 Apr. 1944
Bennington (CV-20)	Newport News	15 Dec. 1942	26 Feb. 1944	6 Aug. 1944
Boxer (CV-21)	Newport News	13 Sep. 1943	14 Dec. 1944	16 Apr. 1945
Bon Homme Richard (CV-31)	New York	1 Feb. 1943	29 Apr. 1944	26 Nov. 1944
Leyte (CV-32)	Newport News	21 Feb. 1944	23 Aug. 1945	11 Apr. 1946
Kearsarge (CV-33)	New York	1 Mar. 1944	5 May 1945	2 Mar. 1946
Oriskany (CV-34)	New York	1 May 1944	13 Oct. 1945	25 Sep. 1950
Reprisal (CV-35)	New York	1 Jul. 1944	Not Launched	
Antietam (CV-36)	Philadelphia	15 Mar. 1943	20 Aug. 1944	28 Jan. 1945
Princeton (CV-37)	Philadelphia	14 Sep. 1943	8 Jul. 1945	18 Nov. 1945
Shangri-La (CV-38)	Norfolk	15 Jan. 1943	24 Feb. 1944	15 Sep. 1944
Lake Champlain (CV-39)	Norfolk	15 Mar. 1943	2 Nov. 1944	3 Jun. 1945
Tarawa (CV-40)	Norfolk	1 Mar. 1944	12 May 1945	8 Dec. 1945
Valley Forge (CV-45)	Philadelphia	7 Sep. 1944	18 Nov. 1945	3 Nov. 1946
Iwo Jima (CV-46)	Philadelphia	29 Jan. 1945	Not launched	
Philippine Sea (CV-47)	Bethlehem	19 Aug. 1944	5 Sep. 1945	11 May 1946

Chapter One

US Navy Aircraft Carrier Development, 1919-41

The US Navy's early involvement with aviation centred around co-operation with Glenn Curtiss, who by 1910 had developed a successful series of pusher biplanes. It was one of these, flown by a Curtiss pilot, which made the first take-off from the deck of a ship on 14 November 1910 and subsequently the first shipboard landing on 18 January 1911. These events prompted the Navy to place

The first take-off by an aeroplane from a ship occurred on 14 November 1910 when Eugene Ely flew a Curtiss pusher biplane from the temporary platform shown here erected on the bows of the cruiser USS *Birmingham*. (NARA)

Ely was a civilian employed by Glenn Curtiss as a demonstration pilot and on 18 January 1911 he made the first landing on a ship, the cruiser USS *Pennsylvania* anchored in San Francisco Bay. In this case the flying platform was erected on the ship's stern and after his successful landing, Ely then took off again – the momentous event being captured in this photograph. (NARA)

an order for the Curtiss machines and the first of these was delivered in July 1911, and by 1914 several aircraft were available for deployment. The US entered the First World War as a combatant nation in 1917 and by 1918 the US Navy and Marine Corps could muster no less than 2,107 aircraft. These included many flying boats as well as aircraft designed to be catapulted from battleships and cruisers.

Despite these advances, the US Navy did not possess any aircraft carriers in 1918 in contrast to the British Royal Navy, which had the world's first aircraft carrier with a full-length flight deck in the shape of HMS *Argus*, a converted liner. There was also HMS *Furious*, a converted battlecruiser with a flying off deck forward and a landing deck aft. Even more significantly, work had begun in January 1918 on the world's first purpose-designed aircraft carrier, HMS *Hermes*, although she was not completed until 1923. Another project underway in 1918 was the conversion of the ex-Chilean battleship *Almirante Cochrane*, which eventually joined the fleet as HMS *Eagle* in 1924.

A squadron of US battleships had served with the British Grand Fleet in 1918 and US naval officers were able to observe at first hand the progress being made in British naval aviation. Consequently, in 1919 the US Navy ordered its first aircraft carrier in the form of a converted collier (USS *Jupiter*) which was completed as the USS *Langley* (CV-1) in 1922. With a maximum speed of only 15 knots, she was not suitable for fleet work but nevertheless enabled the US Navy to gain valuable experience of operating aircraft from a carrier and to develop tactics for their utilisation. It was not until 1928 that two more carriers joined the fleet in the form of the converted battlecruisers USS *Lexington* (CV-2) and USS *Saratoga* (CV-3). These were produced as a result of the 1922 Washington Naval Treaty which required the scrapping of many older capital ships and construction of new larger

The USS *Langley* (CV-1) was the US Navy's first aircraft carrier and she commissioned in March 1922. Originally built as the collier USS *Jupiter* and launched in 1912, she was taken in hand for conversion to an aircraft carrier in 1920. The reconstruction was relatively straightforward with a continuous flight deck being built over the existing superstructure, although the funnels were angled from the port side as shown in this photograph taken in 1928. There was no hangar as such but four of the previous coal holds were adapted for aircraft storage from whence they could be hoisted onto the open main deck under the flight deck, which in turn was reached by means of a centrally located electric lift. On deck are a dozen Vought FU-1 fighter biplanes operated by VF-2B. (NARA)

Between 1922 and 1936 the USS *Langley* provided the US Navy with a very useful platform for training pilots and flight-deck crews, for testing new aircraft and for developing the tactical use of an aircraft carrier and its squadrons. Eventually she operated an air group consisting of twelve fighters, ten torpedo bombers and twelve scout/observation aircraft. However, with the advent of newer and larger carriers she was taken out of service and in 1936–7 converted to an aircraft transport under the designation AV-3, and the forward section of the flight deck was removed. In this guise she is shown delivering a cargo of Consolidated P2Y patrol flying boats belonging to Patrol Squadron VP-19 to Pearl Harbor in 1939. She was subsequently sunk on 27 February 1942 by Japanese aircraft while attempting to deliver USAAF P-40 fighters to Java. (NARA)

vessels to be suspended. Among these were the two battlecruisers which would have displaced 43,500 tons (well in excess of the 35,000-ton limit imposed by the treaty). However, it was agreed that the signatory nations could construct aircraft carriers up to a total of 135,000 tons as long as none exceeded the 35,000-ton limit. Accordingly, the *Lexington* and *Saratoga*, originally laid down in 1920–1, were redesigned and completed as aircraft carriers and commissioned at the end of 1927. The removal of the heavy main armament of eight 16in guns and some of the armour protection resulted in a final standard displacement of 33,000 tons. At the time they were the largest aircraft carriers in the world and remained so until the end of the Second World War when the first of the Midway class commissioned.

It is interesting to note that in the same timescale Japan produced similar conversions using the battlecruiser *Akagi* and battleship *Kagi* while the UK converted the light battlecruisers *Glorious* and *Courageous*.

The first purpose-designed US aircraft carrier was the USS *Ranger* (CV-4) which was laid down in September 1931 and commissioned in July 1934. At 14,000 tons, she was considerably smaller than the two battlecruiser conversions but was capable of carrying almost as many aircraft (up to eighty-six). In fact, she proved too small for sustained operational use in the Second World War and apart from supporting the invasion of North Africa (Operation Torch) in November 1942, she was employed mainly as an aircraft transport or training carrier. The much-reduced displacement

USS *Lexington* (CV-2) commissioned in December 1927 and is seen here running trials the following year. Originally laid down in 1921 as one of a class of large 43,000-ton battlecruisers to be armed with eight 16in guns, under the provisions of the 1922 Washington Treaty all were cancelled or scrapped apart from *Lexington* and her sister ship *Saratoga*, which were both completed as aircraft carriers. The original lines of the battlecruiser hull are evident in this view and the huge funnel contains the uptakes for the twenty-four boilers which provided steam for the 180,000shp turbo-electric machinery. These endowed the ships with a speed of 33 knots, making them the fastest aircraft carriers in world at that time. (NARA)

Above: One unusual aspect the Lexington class carriers was that they were armed with a battery of eight 8in guns mounted in twin turrets fore and aft of the central island. At the time of their conversion it was thought necessary for carriers to be able to defend themselves against potential surface attack by enemy cruisers. These here form a backdrop to a busy flight deck scene in 1940 as a Grumman F4F Wildcat prepares to take off. In practice the guns could only have been fired to starboard as firing to port across the flight deck would prevent flying operations and the blast could damage parked aircraft. (NARA)

Opposite above: The USS *Saratoga* (CV-3) was actually laid down and completed before its sister ship, *Lexington*. Commissioned on 16 November 1927, she is shown here preparing to enter the Panama Canal in 1930 after participating in the Presidential Naval Review at Norfolk VA. With a beam of 104ft 7in (31.88m), she was a tight fit in the canal locks which until recently were only 110ft wide. Again, the battlecruiser origins of these vessels are clearly apparent. (NARA)

Opposite below: An overhead view of USS *Saratoga* in May 1932 with flying operations in progress. There are over fifty aircraft parked well forward to allow aircraft to land on the after section of the flight deck. A safety barrier would be raised as each aircraft landed to prevent it running into the deck park if it missed the arrester wires. The landing aircraft in this case are Great Lakes TG-2 torpedo bombers operated by VT-2B. Earlier that year *Saratoga* and *Lexington* had launched a successful surprise dawn strike against Pearl Harbor during Grand Joint Exercise No. 4. Little was it realised that the Japanese Navy would do exactly the same thing some nine years later. (NARA)

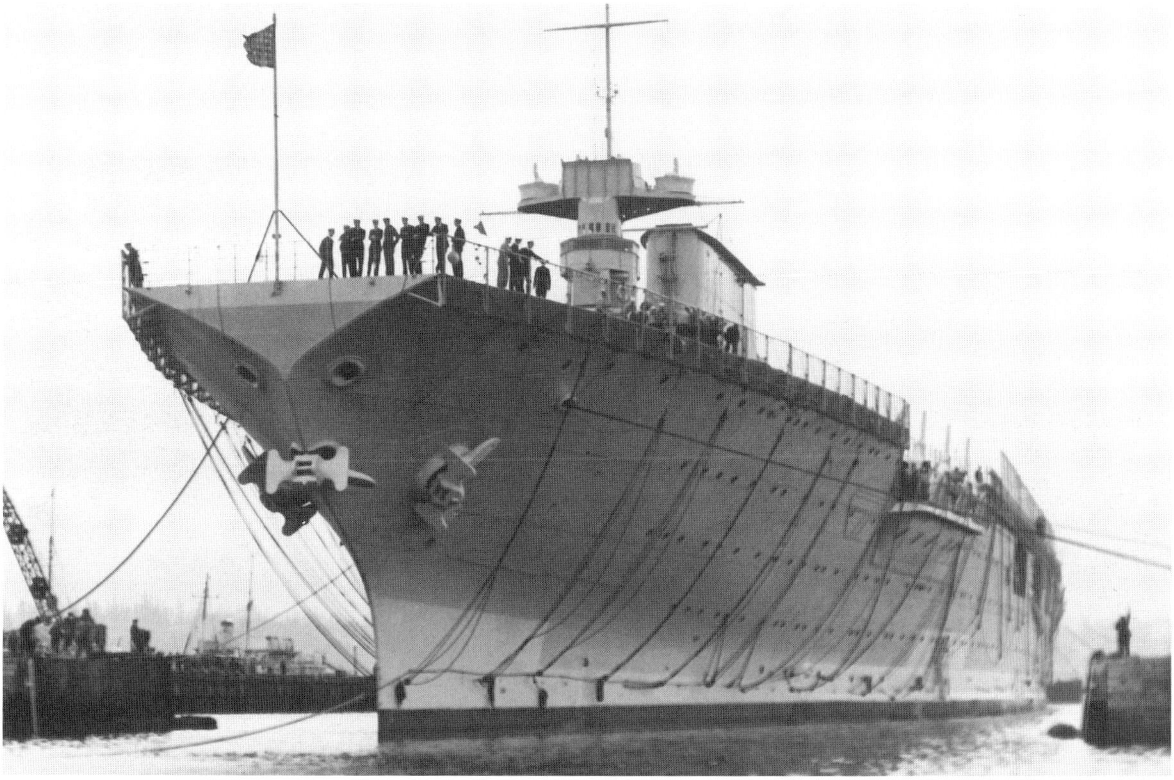

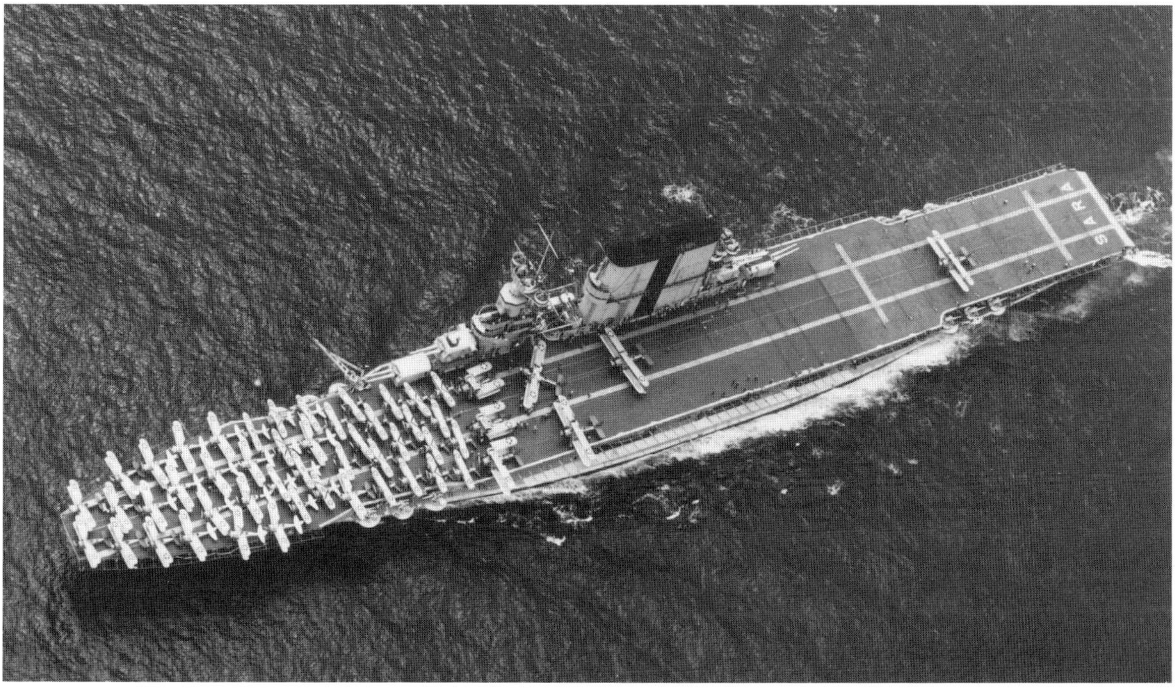
SARA

was partially a consequence of the Washington Treaty as building a small carrier left enough available tonnage for subsequent larger carriers. These were the Yorktown class which displaced 19,800 tons (standard) and were based on the *Ranger* but with enlarged overall dimensions and the boiler uptakes faired into a single funnel incorporated in the island superstructure (*Ranger* had an awkward arrangement of three funnels on either side of the after flight deck which could be lowered to a horizontal position during flying operations).

Above: The US Navy's first purpose-built aircraft carrier was the USS *Ranger* (CV-4), which was laid down on 26 September 1931 and launched on 25 February 1933. She is shown here fitting out later in 1933 at the Newport yard where she was built. Work is in progress to lay the wooden flight deck and the small island superstructure is taking shape, the latter being something of an afterthought as it was not a feature of the original design. Starting with a clean-sheet design, the emphasis was very much on the aviation facilities and although displacing only 14,000 tons, less than half the displacement of the Lexington class, she could in theory accommodate the same number of aircraft (eighty). (NARA)

Opposite above: The USS *Ranger* commissioned on 4 July 1934 and is shown here as completed. A notable feature is the six funnels arranged either side of the after flight deck and these could be lowered to the horizontal position during flight operations. Also apparent is the fact that the hangars and flight deck are separate structures built over the main deck. In practice her small size proved to be a liability, flight operations were unduly affected by poor weather conditions and with a speed of only 29 knots she could not combine tactically with the larger carriers. Consequently her wartime service was restricted to the Atlantic theatre where she supported the North Africa landings in November 1942 and later worked with the British Home Fleet in 1944 before being relegated to training duties. (NARA)

The US Navy's Pacific Fleet carriers anchored off Honolulu in the spring of 1938. In the foreground is the USS *Ranger* with over sixty aircraft ranged on deck. Behind her is the USS *Lexington* and furthest from the camera is the USS *Saratoga*, distinguishable by the vertical black stripe on her funnel. These ships had recently completed a series of fleet exercises which again had included a dawn attack on Pearl Harbor and other installations. (NARA)

The new carriers, *Yorktown* (CV-5) and *Enterprise* (CV-6), were laid down in 1934 and commissioned in September 1937 and May 1938 respectively. Theoretically capable of operating up to ninety-six aircraft, they more commonly embarked about eighty to facilitate more efficient handling. Both proved very successful in service and *Enterprise* featured prominently in the naval battles of 1942 and survived to serve throughout the Second World War, although her sister ship, *Yorktown*, was lost at Midway in June 1942. In 1936 the US Navy was still subject to the Washington Treaty tonnage limitations and following on from the laying down of the Yorktown class had only 15,000 tons available for a further carrier. This was laid down in April 1936 as the USS *Wasp* (CV-7), which commissioned in April 1940. Standard displacement was reduced to just under 15,000 tons by reducing the length of the hull and flight deck, installing less powerful machinery driving only two shafts (Yorktown class had four shafts) and eliminating virtually all armour protection. Nevertheless, she was capable of operating up to seventy-six aircraft.

Originally it had been planned to build five of the small Ranger class carriers, as the best way of utilising the tonnage available under the Washington Treaty. However, even while the USS *Ranger* was under construction the limitations of a relatively small carrier were recognised and in August 1933 the navy was authorised to begin work on two new 20,000-ton carriers. The first of these was the USS *Yorktown* (CV-5), which laid down at Newport News in May 1934 and eventually commissioned on 20 September 1937. They were designed to accommodate up to ninety-six aircraft and the 120,000shp steam-turbine machinery gave the ship a speed of 32.5 knots. (NARA)

This aerial view of the USS *Yorktown* shortly after completion shows to advantage the layout of the flight deck with identifying code letters at either end. It was US Navy policy at the time that aircraft carriers should be able to recover aircraft while going astern and so arrester wires, visible in this photo, are installed across the bow section of the flight deck. The Yorktown class were equipped to handle an air group of no less than 96 aircraft comprising 18 fighters, 36 torpedo bombers, 37 dive bombers and 5 utility aircraft. The latter were typically Grumman J2F amphibians of the type seen here parked on deck. (NARA)

Above: USS *Enterprise* (CV-6) was the second ship of the Yorktown class and commissioned in May 1938. This photo shows her lying in the James River on 6 April 1938 while undergoing contractor's trials. Despite the increased size, the design of the ship echoed features of the *Ranger* with the flight deck and hangars built as superstructure rather than as an integral part of the hull, as was the practice with contemporary British aircraft carriers. For self-defence a battery of eight single 5in DP guns were carried in pairs quadrantally disposed at the fore and aft edges of the flight deck. (NARA)

Opposite above: *Enterprise* secured alongside North Island Naval Air Station (NAS) at San Diego embarking her aircraft, which were towed along the road from the airfield to the jetty and then hoisted aboard by crane. At that time her air group comprised 16 Grumman F3F fighters of VF-6, 18 Curtiss SBC Helldivers of VS-6, 15 Northrop BT dive bombers of VB-6 and 16 Douglas TBD Devastators of VT-6. It is significant to note the relatively small number of fighters embarked and wartime experience was to show the need to substantially increase their numbers. Affectionately known as the 'Big E', *Enterprise* was to have an extremely active war, participating in many major actions including the final assault on Japan. (NARA)

Opposite below: Having laid down the *Yorktown* and *Enterprise*, the US Navy had only 15,000 tons available for a further carrier under the limitations of the Washington Treaty. This dictated the size of the next carrier which was laid down in April 1936 as the USS *Wasp* (CV-7). Although the design was based on that of the preceding class, in order to reduce tonnage several compromises had to be accepted. These included a shorter hull and flight deck, two shaft machinery for a speed of 29.5 knots, no armour protection and, significantly, no anti-torpedo protection. Maximum aircraft capacity was reduced to seventy-six. (NARA)

13

Wasp was fated to have a short but eventful career after commissioning in April 1940. In 1941 she flew off thirty USAAF P-40 fighters as part of the American occupation of Iceland and in early 1942 she formed part of a US task force operating with the British Home Fleet based at Scapa Flow. During that time, she made two deployments to the Mediterranean to fly off RAF Spitfires to beleaguered Malta. This view of *Wasp* was taken from the British Cruiser HMS *Edinburgh* in March 1942 as she joined the Home Fleet. By June 1942 she had returned to the US for a short refit before deploying to the Pacific where she was sorely needed. (NARA)

The Washington Treaty lapsed in October 1936 and the London Naval Treaty of that year placed no restriction on permissible tonnage for aircraft carriers. However, it was not until 1937 that Congress approved the construction of up to 40,000 tons of carrier, and while the design of what would become the new Essex class was still being finalised, the decision was taken to order a further Yorktown class in the shape of the USS *Hornet* (CV-8). Laid down in September 1939, she commissioned on 10 October 1941 – only three weeks before Pearl Harbor. Thus, on that fateful day the US Navy had available seven aircraft carriers (the USS *Langley* had been converted for use as a seaplane tender and aircraft transport and the forward section of her flight deck had been removed). Over the next twelve months these carriers saw intensive action and four of them were sunk before the end of 1942, while the badly damaged *Enterprise* was undergoing major repairs. With the USS *Ranger* deployed

Restrictions on the total tonnage of aircraft carriers permitted to each navy were dropped in 1937 and, with a deteriorating international situation, an expansion of the US carrier fleet was approved. Although the design of the new Essex class carriers was in progress, it was decided to build a further ship of the Yorktown class as this could be placed in service at a much earlier date. Accordingly, the USS *Hornet* (CV-8) was laid down in September 1939 and was commissioned just over two years later in October 1941, only a few weeks before the Pearl Harbor attack brought the US into the Second World War. She differed in detail from her sister ships in that her flight deck was slightly wider and her light anti-aircraft armament was boosted by four quadruple 1.1in AA guns and twenty-four single 0.5in machine guns. This photo was taken in October 1941 around the time the ship commissioned but at that point the single 5in guns and some of the 1.1in mountings had yet to be fitted. (NARA)

in the Atlantic, only the USS *Saratoga* was available for Pacific operations, although in early 1943 she was briefly supported by the Royal Navy carrier HMS *Victorious* which had been made available following a request from the US Navy. However, relief was at a hand as the new Essex class carriers became available in significant numbers from the middle of 1943, enabling the creation of naval task forces which would spearhead the advance across the Pacific. The vital work of the early carriers that had been lost in action (*Lexington*, *Yorktown*, *Wasp* and *Hornet*) was honoured as four of the Essex class were launched bearing those illustrious names.

Above: In April 1942 the USS *Hornet* joined with USS *Enterprise* to form Task Force 16, the objective of which was to launch a force of USAAF B-25 Mitchell bombers for a daring raid against targets in and around Tokyo. The bombers are shown here ranged on the deck of the *Hornet* while fighters from *Enterprise* provided air cover for the force which included four cruisers and eight destroyers. Launched on 18 April, the bombers achieved complete surprise and although the material damage inflicted was minimal the raid provided a substantial boost to national morale and caused the Japanese to divert vital resources to home defence. (NARA)

Opposite above: The Battle of the Coral Sea was the first to be fought entirely by carrier based aircraft. On 7 May 1942 US Navy aircraft sank the Japanese light carrier *Shoho* but the next day Japanese aircraft found and attacked the USS *Lexington*, which was hit by three torpedoes and two bombs. Initially the damage was contained, and she even resumed flying operations for a while. However, fires continued to burn and eventually the ship was wracked by two major explosions causing even more fires which ran out of control. With the ship listing heavily, she was abandoned and later finished off by torpedoes from a US destroyer. Amazingly, although 216 of her crew were lost, no less than 2,735 men were saved. However, the loss of this fine ship was a severe blow. (NARA)

Opposite below: After frantic efforts to repair damage incurred during the Battle of the Coral Sea the USS *Yorktown* was patched up enough to join *Enterprise* and *Hornet* in time to participate in the Battle of Midway on 4 June 1942, and her dive bombers scored hits on some of the Japanese carriers lost that day. However, she was in turn attacked by Japanese dive bombers, which scored three serious hits and although initially the ship effected repairs, in a later attack she was hit by two torpedoes. The crew initially abandoned ship but as she stayed afloat a salvage party went aboard on 6 June to try and save the ship but their efforts were dramatically halted when she was hit by two torpedoes from a Japanese submarine. The salvage crew was evacuated and the *Yorktown* finally rolled over and sank early the following morning. Here the *Yorktown* is seen on 6 June while the salvage crew was aboard and with one of several destroyers which were attempting to screen the stricken ship. (NARA)

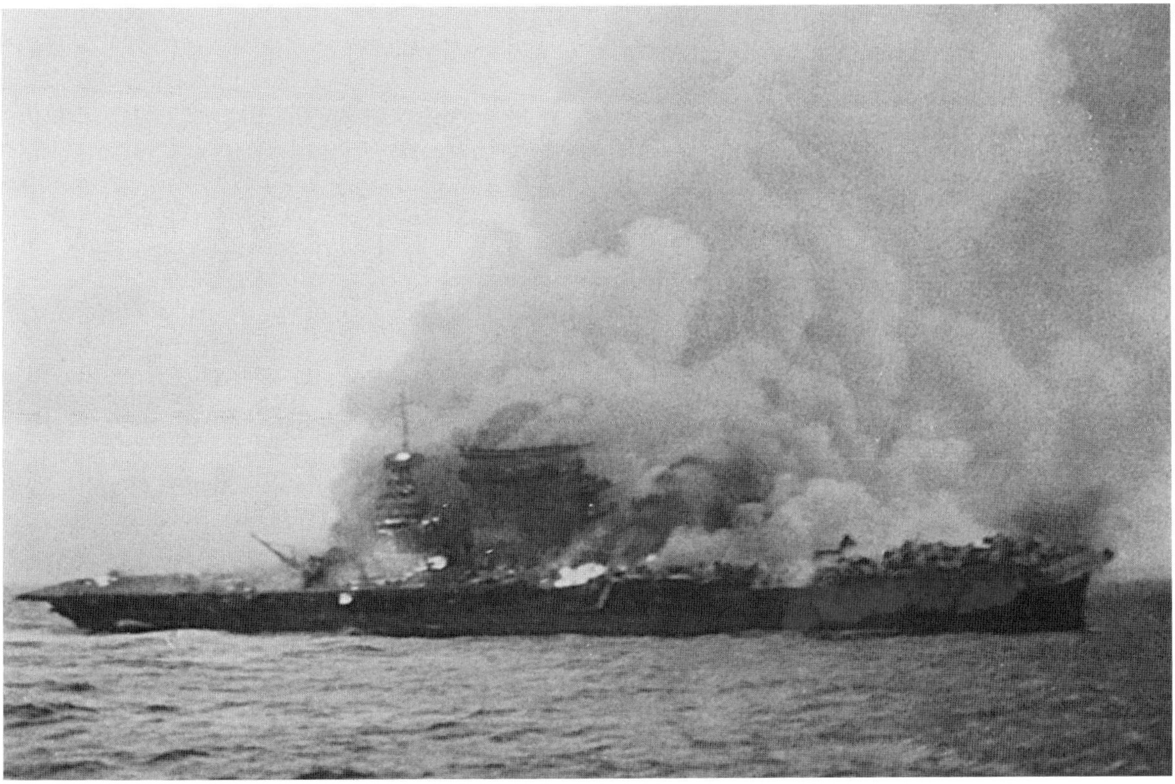

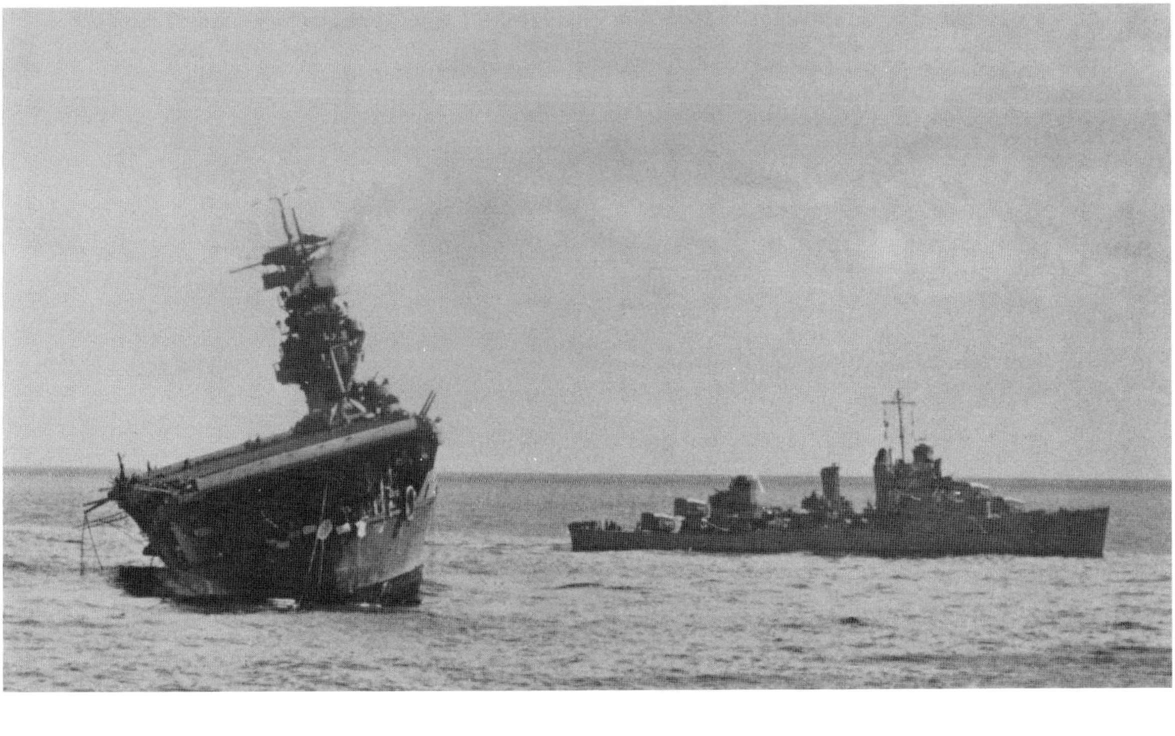

Above: The USS *Wasp* on fire on 15 September 1942 after being struck by three torpedoes fired from the Japanese submarine I-19. At the time *Wasp* was part of a task force escorting transports carrying USMC troops to reinforce those already in action on Guadalcanal. The torpedoes hit at around 1445 and a series of explosions started raging fires which could not be brought under control. Consequently, just over 30 minutes later, the order was given to 'abandon ship', which was done in an orderly manner. By evening the ship was still afloat but burning furiously with violent explosions still occurring. Consequently, the destroyer USS *Lansdowne* was ordered to finish her off with torpedoes and she finally sank at 2100 that evening. Of her crew, 196 were killed but 1,946 (including over 300 wounded) were rescued. (NARA)

Opposite above: On 26 October US and Japanese carriers clashed again in the Battle of Santa Cruz, another episode in the long, drawn-out Guadalcanal campaign. In this battle *Hornet* was attacked mid-morning and took several bomb and torpedo hits which brought her to a standstill. Later she was taken under tow by the cruiser *Northampton* but in the late afternoon another air attack developed, and she was hit with more torpedoes and bombs. Consequently, the ship was abandoned but attempts to sink her by gunfire and torpedoes from US destroyers had little effect and it was left to the advancing Japanese surface force to finish her off during the night. This dramatic image shows her under attack from a Val dive bomber during the morning action. The USS *Enterprise* was seriously damaged at Santa Cruz and was withdrawn for temporary repairs but was in action again in November but with her forward lift still inoperable. (NARA)

By early 1943 the USS *Saratoga* was the only serviceable fast carrier available to the US Navy in the Pacific (*Enterprise* was undergoing a much-needed refit). Following an earlier request, the Royal Navy was able to deploy the carrier HMS *Victorious* to the Pacific where she joined with *Saratoga* to provide cover for the invasion of New Georgia in June 1943. For this operation she had an air group of RN and USN Wildcat fighter squadrons and was responsible for the air defence of the operation as her radar and fighter direction facilities were superior to those of the US carrier. This arrangement was not seriously tested as the Japanese air opposition was negligible and, at the end of July, she left the area en route for home. By that time four of the new Essex class carriers were in commission as well as several of the smaller Independence class light fleet carriers – the tide was about to turn! (NARA)

Chapter Two

Essex Class Enter Service

The lapsing of the naval treaties at the end of 1936 freed the US Navy from the artificial tonnage limitations and allowed the design of a new class of carriers which could be optimised for their intended roles without being driven by the requirement to remain within a set displacement. In 1937 Congress had approved 40,000 tons of carrier construction and two new carriers, the first of which was the USS *Hornet* (CV-8) and the second was to be the USS *Essex* (CV-9), which acted as the prototype for the new design. Initially this was to be a repeat of the Yorktown with minor modifications. However, the US Navy sought to build on its experience with the earlier carriers but required a 10 per cent increase in aircraft capacity, a longer and wider flight deck to facilitate aircraft handling, a 25 per cent increase in spares and stores to allow prolonged combat operations, improved protection against bombs and torpedoes, and a substantial increase in anti-aircraft firepower. While much of this was achieved, it came at a price and standard displacement rose to 27,200 tons (compared with the 20,000-ton Yorktown class), but by the time the Essex was ordered in February 1940 any thought of restricting displacement had disappeared.

As completed, the Essex was 50ft longer and had a 10ft greater beam at the waterline while the flight deck with overall dimensions of 872ft by 96ft was 70ft longer and 10ft wider than the Yorktown class. Another innovation that improved aircraft handling was the introduction of a deck-edge lift amidships which could be folded to a vertical position for transit through the Panama Canal. The disposition of the main anti-aircraft armament was another obvious improvement. This comprised a total of twelve 5in/38cal DP guns of which eight were disposed in four twin mountings carried in superimposed positions fore and aft of the island superstructure. The remaining four guns were disposed in pairs of single open mountings below the forward and after edges of the port-side flight deck. Ships of the Essex class were among the first to receive the new 40mm AA gun which was carried in eight quadruple mountings.

The original aircraft complement was set at 36 fighters, 37 dive bombers (the odd aircraft was allocated to the air group commander to act as leader in air strikes) and 18 torpedo bombers making a total of 91. Later in the war this total was often exceeded, sometimes with more than 100 aircraft being embarked.

The Essex class carriers represented a significant step forward in carrier design and several were named after other carriers which had been lost earlier in the war. This photograph of the new USS *Yorktown* (CV-10), taken in July 1944, shows the spacious flight deck, longer and wider than its predecessors, and also the deck-edge lift on the port side, opposite the island superstructure. At the time the ship was engaged in strikes supporting troops ashore on Saipan (Operation Forager) and ranged on deck are F6F Hellcats of VF-1 and SB2C Helldivers of VB-1. (NARA)

The traditional bottle of champagne is broken over the bow of USS *Essex* (CV-9) as she is about to be launched on 31 July 1942. The lady wielding the bottle is Mrs Alice Gates who was the wife of Artemus Gates, the then Assistant Secretary of the Navy for Air. Note the two men in the foreground, apparently ready to give the 27,000-ton carrier a helping hand down the slipway! (NHHC)

Two more Essex class were ordered in July 1940 but following the fall of France Congress had already passed the Two-Ocean Naval Act which authorised a substantial increase in the strength of the US Navy. This resulted in orders for a further ten Essex class while after America's entry into the war orders for a further nineteen were authorised, although some of these were not completed until after 1945 and six were cancelled altogether. Nevertheless, eventually no fewer than twenty-four Essex class carriers were completed (all except six before the end of the Second World War), a building programme unmatched by any of the other naval powers. The tide of war in the Pacific was ultimately turned in America's favour by its industrial might, building some individual Essex class carriers in as short a time as eighteen months

Essex was one of no less than ten other vessels of the same class to be built by the Newport News Shipbuilding and Dry Dock Company. Here shipyard works and navy personnel watch as she slides gracefully into the water. Fitting out was achieved within the short time of five months and the ship was commissioned on 31 December 1942. (NHHC)

from keel laying to commissioning. And it was not only in terms of ships that the US Navy was ahead of the Imperial Japanese Navy. Both sides suffered severe losses of experienced aircrew in the 1942 carrier battles, but the US had the manpower and organisation to produce an ever increasing flow of well-trained replacements needed to man its ever expanding carrier fleet, whereas the Japanese never made up their early losses and replacements were not as well trained.

The Essex class carriers were named after events and ships associated with US history, notably the War of Independence in 1776 and the War of 1812 as well as the American Civil War. Others commemorated some of the carriers lost in 1942 and later ships were named after Second World War battles. Essex herself was named after a thirty-six-gun sail frigate which had a successful career in the War of 1812 before being captured after a fierce fight with two British ships in 1814.

The new aircraft carriers were referred to as the Essex class after the lead ship laid down on 28 April 1941. In fact, she was the fourth US Navy ship to bear that name. The first was a sail frigate launched in 1799, the second a steam river ferry launched in 1856 but in 1861 converted into an ironclad gun boat for the Federal Navy which saw action in the American Civil War. The third was a steam frigate launched in 1874 and pictured here towards the end of the nineteenth century when she was acting as a training ship for US Navy cadets from Annapolis. (NARA)

Above: In May 1943, after official trials and working up with a new air group, USS *Essex* was ready for action and is shown as she set off from Hampton Roads for a transit through the Panama Canal in order to join the Pacific Fleet at Pearl Harbor. On deck are 24 SBD scout bombers parked aft, a dozen F6F fighters and about eighteen TBF/TBM torpedo planes parked amidships. These belonged to Air Group 9 which had an overall strength of ninety aircraft. (NARA)

Opposite above: USS *Yorktown* was also built at Newport News and was launched on 21 January 1943. She was actually laid down on 1 December 1941 as the USS *Bon Homme Richard* but the name was changed while under construction to commemorate the earlier *Yorktown* (CV-5) sunk at the Battle of Midway. (NARA)

Opposite below: Essex class carriers had an official complement of 2,682 officers and men and a substantial proportion of those, together with friends and family, are paraded on deck at the formal commissioning of the USS *Yorktown* at Norfolk Naval Yard on 15 April 1943. With a full air group embarked the number of men on board would rise to around 3,500. Prominent in this view are the after pair of twin 5in/38cal DP gun mountings and above those are two quadruple 40mm AA mountings. A similar arrangement was in place at the forward end of the island superstructure. (NARA)

25

26

Above: As the new carriers were completed and commissioned, they were deployed to the Pacific where they joined the Fast Carrier Task Forces which would play such a vital role in the advance across the ocean towards Japan itself. During the period when the task forces were building up and no major operations were in progress the capacity of the large hangar and flight deck was often utilised for the transport of the troops and equipment which would be needed for the planned assaults on the island groups of the Central Pacific. In this case some of the 2,500 troops embarked in *Yorktown* in September 1943 en route from the US West Coast to Hawaii are accommodated in cots spread out on the hangar deck. (NARA)

Opposite above: USS *Yorktown* in November 1943 while forming part of TG 50.1 during Operation Galvanic – the invasion of the Gilbert Islands. At that time she had Air Group 5 embarked equipped with F6F fighters, SBD dive bombers and TBF torpedo bombers, and one of the fighters can be seen over the round down about to land. In the bow section the hangar side screens are open and an SBD can be seen within. The facility to open the hangar sides improved ventilation and allowed aircraft to run up their engines in the hangar. (NARA)

Opposite below: The influence that the Essex class carriers were to have on the course of the Pacific War was not just a function of their increased size and efficiency. Their entry into service also coincided with the introduction of new and improved aircraft of which the Grumman F6F Hellcat, here aboard *Yorktown* in 1943, was perhaps the most significant. Until that time the mainstay of the US Navy's fighter strength was the F4F Wildcat which, although a sturdy and reliable aircraft, was outperformed by the Japanese Zero fighter. The Hellcat was 50mph faster, had almost twice the rate of climb and later versions could carry a pair of 1,000lb bombs enabling it to double up in the strike role. (NARA)

Above: USS *Intrepid* (CV-11) was the last of an initial batch of three Essex class carriers laid down at the Newport News shipyard in 1941 and was launched on 26 April 1943. This view shows that even at that stage the ship was substantially complete. Subsequent work involved detailed fitting out of compartments and the addition of the armament of twelve 5in guns and their associated fire-control equipment. In addition, there would be eight quadruple 40mm AA mountings as well as numerous single 20mm guns. (NARA)

Opposite above: The day after launch, *Intrepid* was moved by tugs to a fitting out berth where she can be seen still carrying the patriotic colours which adorned the ship for the launch. Note the forward lift placed on the flight deck ready for installation in its well during the fitting out process. (NARA)

Opposite below: Intrepid commissioned on 16 August 1943, less than four months after being launched, and is shown lying in Hampton Roads on that date. As with all the early Essex class, she was completed wearing the Measure 21 colour scheme which was an overall dark-blue/grey while the wooden flight deck was painted dark grey. The censor has been at pains to hide details of the radar antenna which actually included the bedstead antenna of the SK search radar above the funnel and SC-2 and SM radars on the tripod foremast. (NARA)

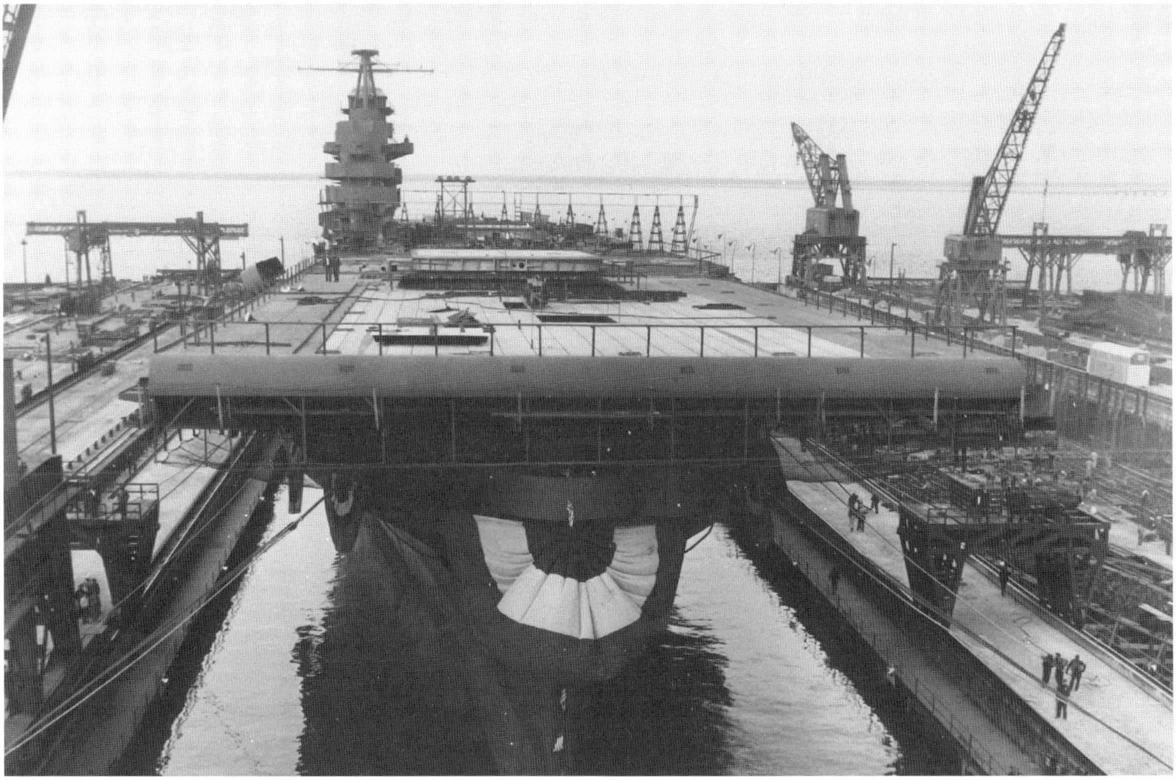

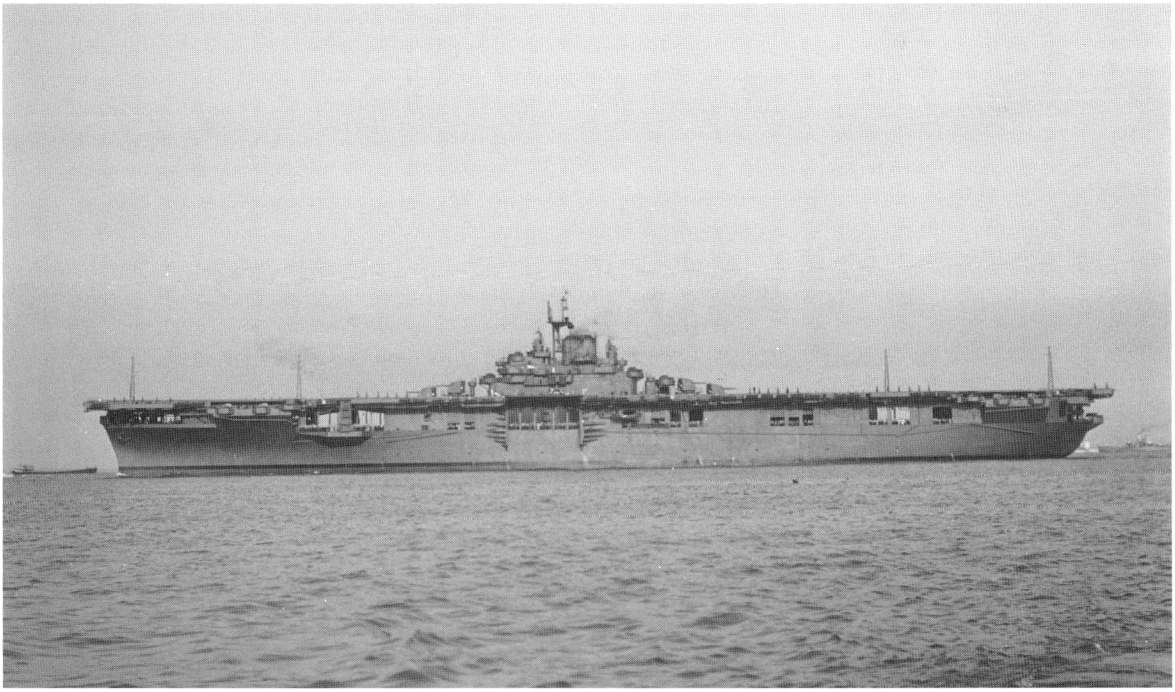

Above: Apart from the three carriers laid down at Newport News, another pair were also laid down in 1941 at the Bethlehem Shipbuilding Corporation's Fore River Shipyard at Quincy MA. The first of these was USS *Lexington* (CV-16), which was laid down on 15 September 1941 and launched just over one year later on 26 September 1942. Originally ordered as the USS *Cabot*, the name was changed to commemorate the previous *Lexington* (CV-2) which was lost at the Battle of the Coral Sea and, coincidently, was also built at the Fore River Shipyard. The name Cabot was later allocated to an Independence class light fleet carrier (CVL-28). (NARA)

Opposite above: The new *Lexington* was commissioned on 17 February 1943, almost exactly eighteen months since she had been laid down and was an excellent illustration of the capabilities of US industrial strength – something that the Japanese (and Germans) could not match. Here the ship makes her way across a frozen Boston harbour following the commissioning ceremony. Note that the lift on the port edge of the flight deck is in the raised position. (NARA)

Opposite below: The *Lexington* photographed on 12 November 1943 shortly after leaving Pearl Harbor to take part in Operation Galvanic. On deck are elements of her Air Group 16 equipped with F6F Hellcats, SBD Dauntless and TBF/TBM Avengers. At this stage she wears her original Measure 21 paintwork, although in 1945 this was changed to Measure 12, a two-tone scheme in which the hull up to hangar deck level was Sea Blue and everything above that was Ocean Grey. In fact, *Lexington* was the only wartime Essex class never to receive one of the geometric dazzle-pattern schemes. (NARA)

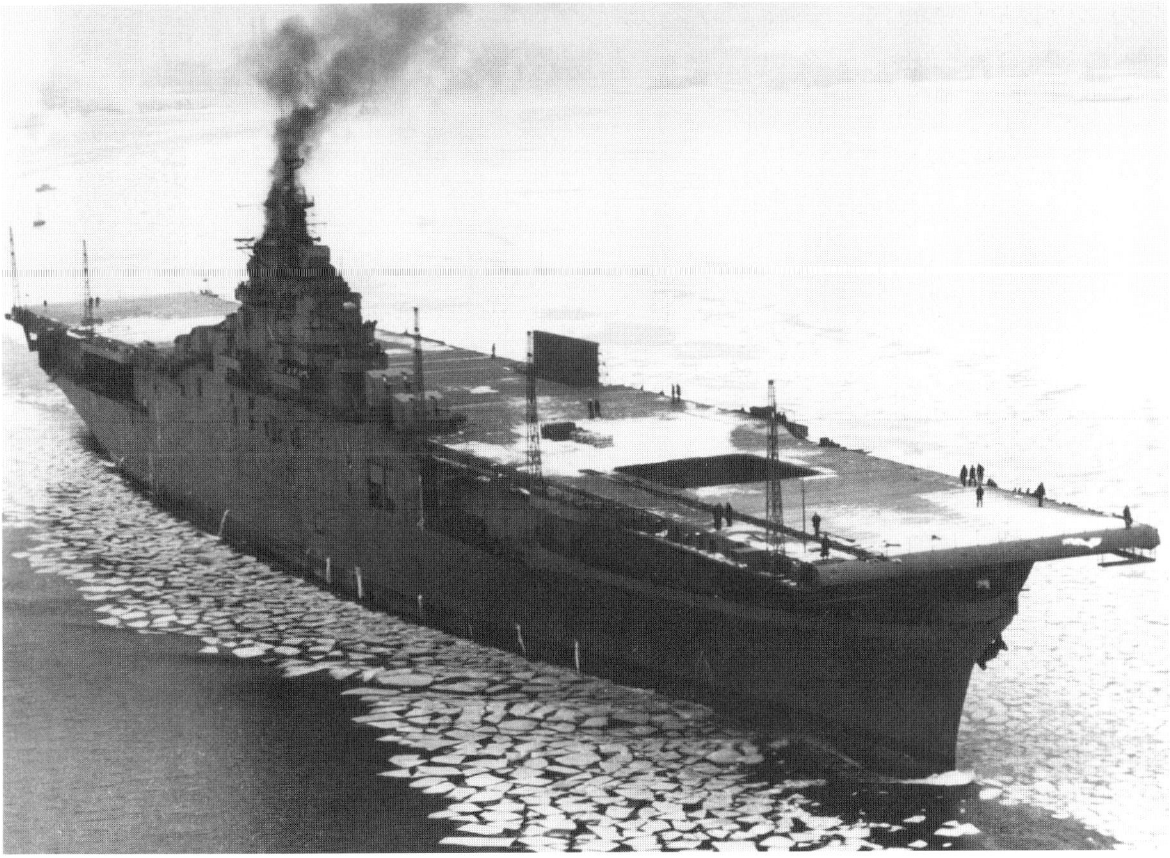

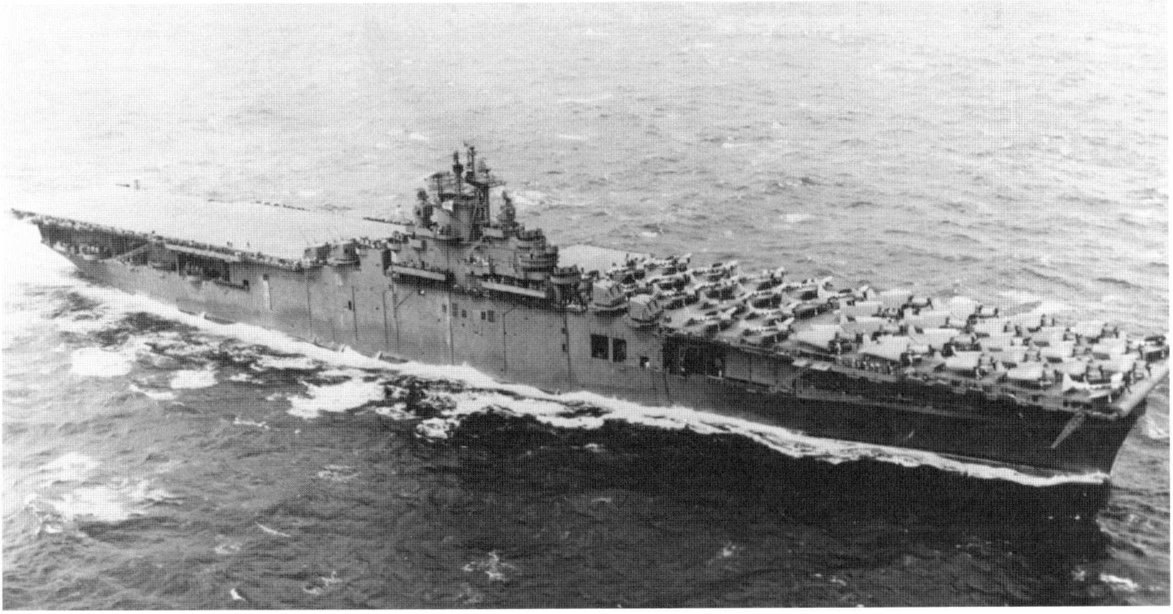

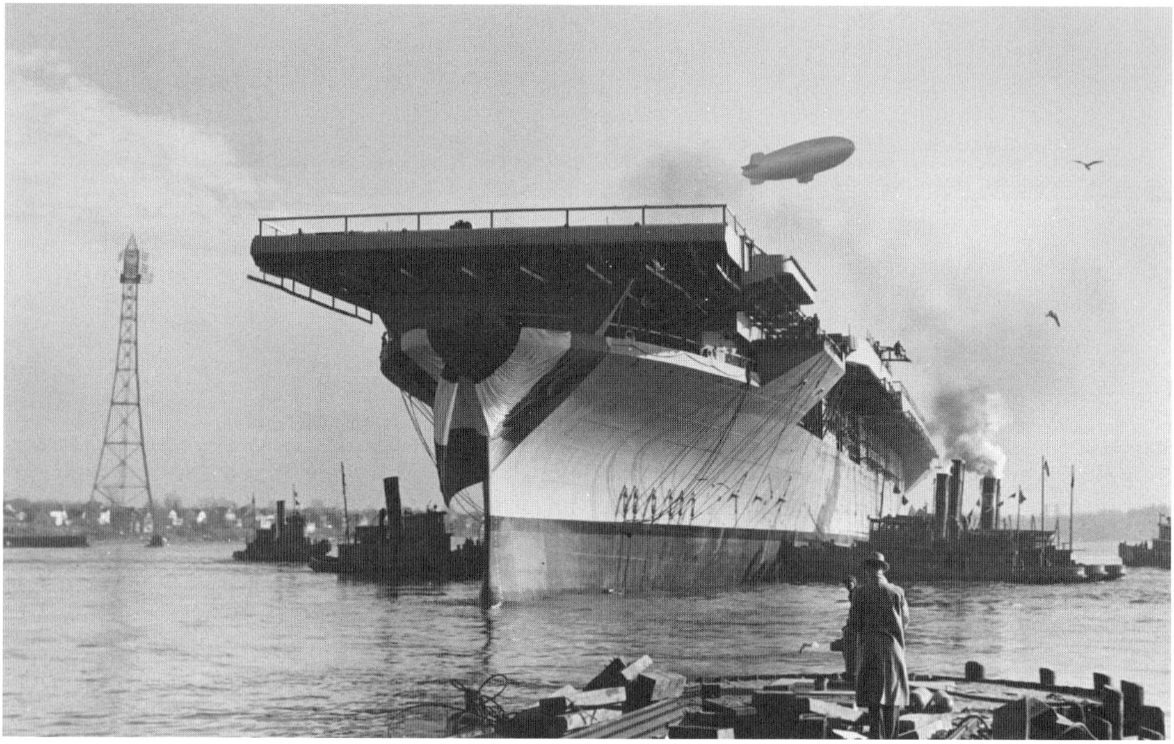

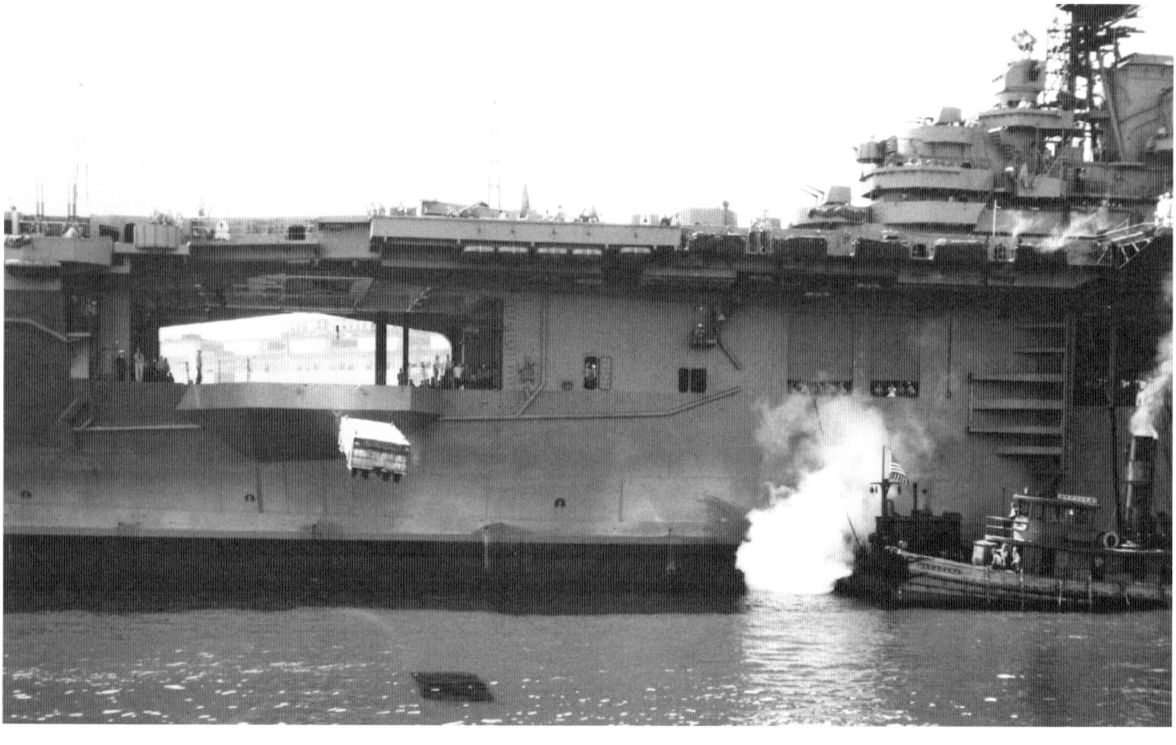

Opposite above: Another launch on the Fore River. This time it is the USS *Bunker Hill* (CV-17) which was laid down on the same day as her sister ship, *Lexington*, and launched on 7 December 1942 (coincidently the first anniversary of Pearl Harbor). *Bunker Hill* would be commissioned on 25 May 1943 and joined the Pacific Fleet at Pearl Harbor towards the end of the following September. (NHHC)

Opposite below: One unusual feature of some of the early Essex class carriers was the provision of a hangar deck catapult to launch aircraft on either beam while a single conventional bow catapult was installed on the flight deck. This arrangement was only fitted to six ships (CVs-10, 11, 12, 13, 17 and 18) but was later removed and a second deck catapult fitted. Here a test load is fired from *Bunker Hill*'s hangar catapult while the ship was fitting out. For aircraft launches an extension track was provided and this could be folded into the vertical position when not in use. This can be seen in the image of USS *Intrepid* on p. 60. (NARA)

After commissioning *Bunker Hill* embarked Air Group 17 (CVG-17) which initially included VF-17 equipped with the new Vought F4U Corsair fighter. With a 2,000hp R-2800 radial engine the F4U-1 Corsair had a maximum speed of 425mph (the first US fighter capable of exceeding 400mph) and would evolve into the most potent of all the Second World War naval fighters. However, its entry into service was less than auspicious due to various factors including a poor view over the long nose for landing and a stiff undercarriage with a tendency to bounce. This is one of VF-17s Corsairs about to take off from *Bunker Hill*'s deck. (NARA)

34

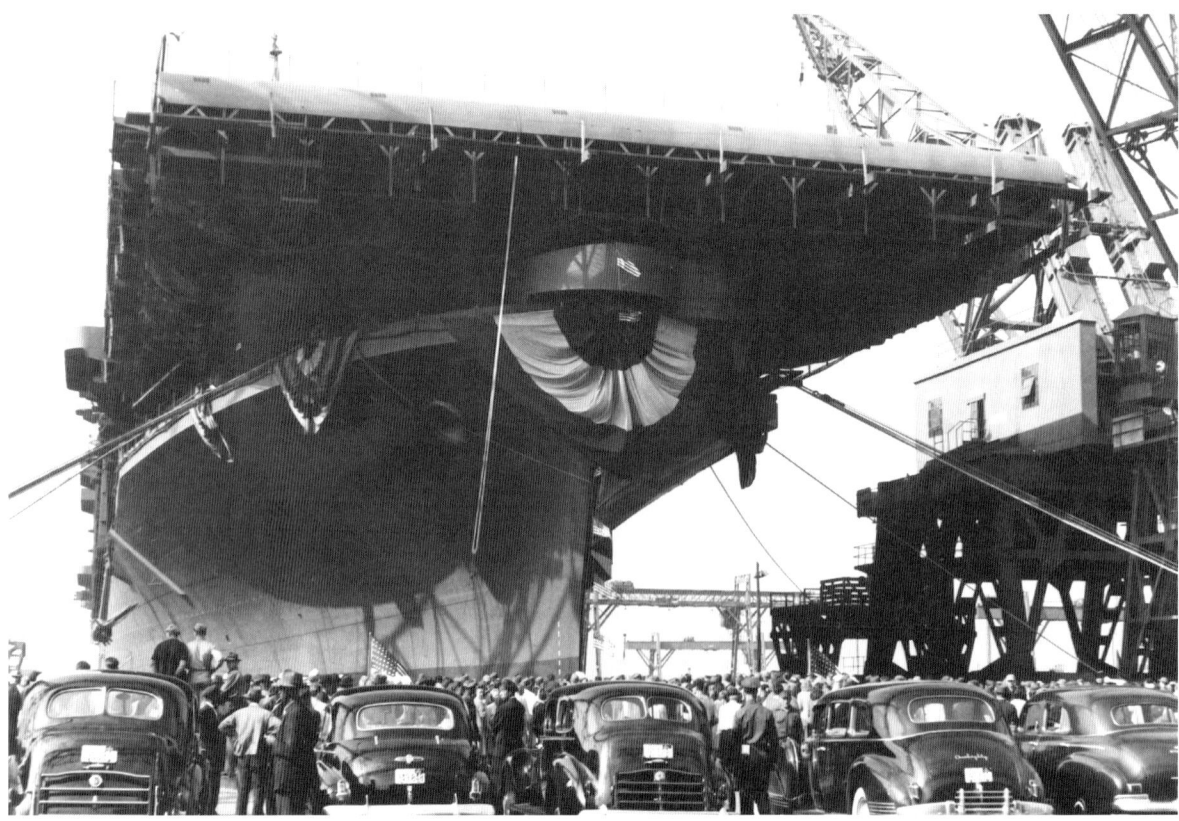

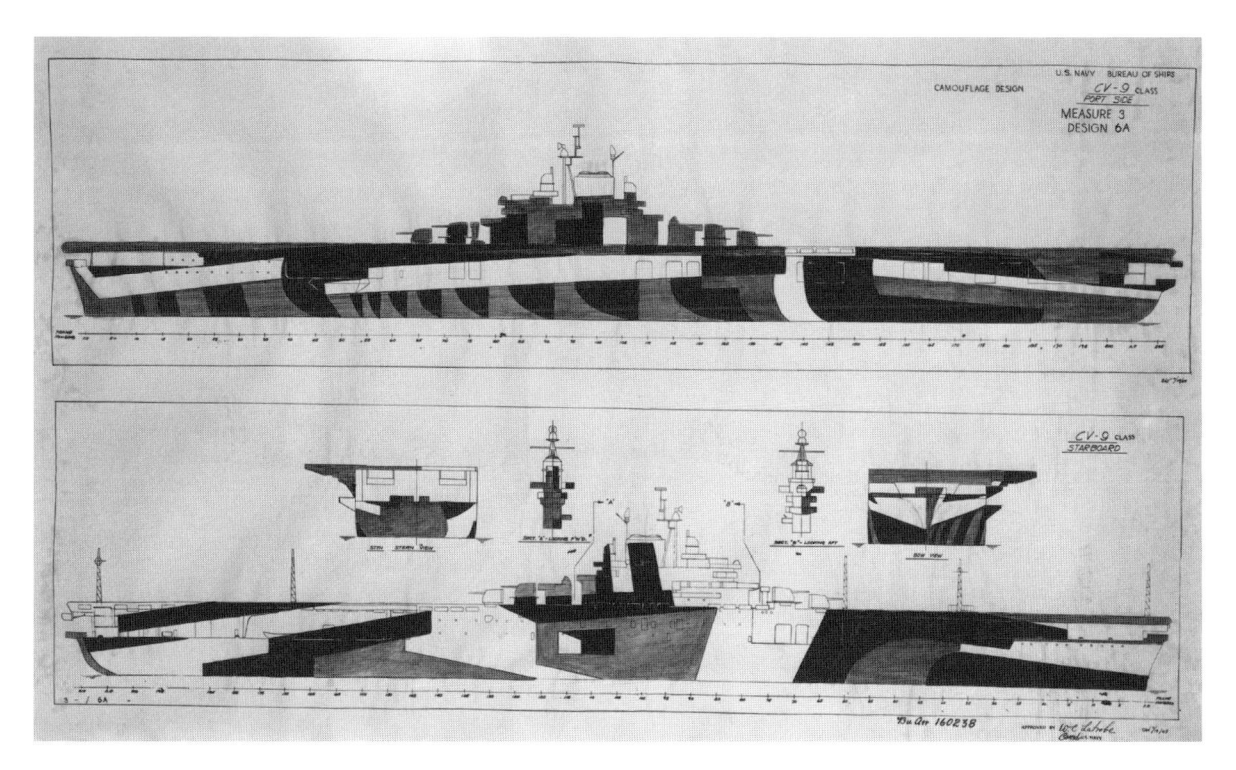

Above: The first six Essex class to complete were finished in the monotone Measure 21 colour scheme but all except *Lexington* later reverted to Measure 32 or 33 dazzle-camouflage schemes, which were also applied to the rest of the wartime construction. This is an official diagram for Measure 32/6A, one of many variations on the basic design. The darker areas are Dull Black or Navy Blue, and the lighter areas various shades of grey. (NARA)

Opposite above: A Corsair about to launch from *Bunker Hill*'s bow catapult. This particular aircraft features the extended tailwheel which was fitted to improve directional stability on landing. However, it still has the original framed canopy and later versions were fitted with a British-inspired bulged frameless canopy which allowed the pilot's seat to be raised and improved all-round visibility. Despite its idiosyncracies, the VF-17 pilots eventually mastered the aircraft and consequently were disappointed when a high-level decision was made to restrict the Corsair to land-based operations and on reaching Pearl Harbor the squadron was landed and eventually deployed to Guadalcanal. It was replaced aboard the ship by the Hellcat equipped VF-18. (NARA)

Opposite below: In 1943 the US Navy commissioned seven Essex class carriers (including CV-12 *Hornet* and CV-15 *Randolph*, not already featured) and another seven in 1944. First among the latter was USS *Franklin* (CV-13). Laid down at Newport News on 7 December 1942, she is shown here ready for launching on 14 October 1943 and was commissioned on 31 January 1944. This was a total build time of less than fourteen months – a staggering achievement. Although there was a Battle of Franklin in the American Civil War, the ship was actually named after Benjamin Franklin, one of the Founding Fathers of the American Republic in 1776. (NARA)

USS *Franklin* leaving Norfolk for a shakedown cruise in the Caribbean before deploying to the Pacific later in the year. She wears the Measure 32/6A camouflage scheme as shown in the previous diagram. The only other ship to be painted in this particular variation was *Bunker Hill* (CV-17). (NARA)

USS *Bunker Hill* in 1944 showing the starboard side of the Measure 32/6A camouflage pattern. (NARA)

Chapter Three

Across the Pacific

After the bruising carrier battles of 1942 and a hard-fought campaign ashore on Guadalcanal, by early 1943 the tide had turned in the Solomons campaign and US and Allied forces were able to begin what would be an arduous and difficult advance towards Rabaul and the recapture of New Guinea. The ultimate aim was to use these locations as a base for the liberation of the Philippines, but this would take almost another two years of fighting. Meanwhile, the US Navy was

A Douglas SBD Dauntless dive bomber of VB-5 from USS *Yorktown* (CV-10) prepares for an attack on Wake Island on 5 October 1943. The SBD Dauntless was a rugged aircraft with excellent low-speed handling characteristics which made it very popular with its aircrews to whom it was universally known as the 'Speedy D'. Clearly visible is the crutch attached to single 1,000lb bomb which enabled it to be swung clear of the propeller arc as it was dropped from a near vertical dive. The Dauntless served in large numbers until phased out of front-line naval service in late 1944, although Marine squadrons continued to fly it until the end of the Pacific War. (NHHC)

gathering its strength for the long-planned advance across the Central Pacific and the new Essex class carriers were essential for this campaign. By August 1943 there were four of them available, supplemented by four of the new Independence class light fleet carriers.

These numbers were not sufficient for an all-out offensive, but in September and October 1943 a number of operations were launched with attacks on Marcus and Wake islands and landings on Baker Island. The Essex class carriers *Essex*, *Yorktown* and *Lexington* were involved in these operations which provided valuable combat experience for the new carriers and their aircrews. In November *Essex* and *Bunker Hill* were dispatched south to cover the landings on Bougainville. Meanwhile, later that month the first major advance took place under the code name Operation Galvanic. Its objective was the capture of the Gilbert Islands and some of the earlier operations had been designed to provide bases which could cover these landings. The main Japanese base was on the island of Tarawa and the US Marines landed there on 20 November 1943. There followed four days of fierce fighting in which the Japanese defended fanatically, almost literally to the last man (from 4,960 troops and construction workers on the island there were only 146 survivors). The US Marines lost just over 1,000 men killed and twice that number wounded. It was a sombre and thought-provoking curtain-raiser to the sort of opposition which could be expected in future assaults, but some lessons were learnt which certainly reduced casualties in future operations (although these would be serious enough). For Operation Galvanic the US Navy was able to deploy four carrier task groups which included the Essex class carriers *Yorktown* and *Lexington* in TG 50.1 and *Essex* and *Bunker Hill* in TG 50.3.

The next objective was the Marshall Islands which included the Kwajalein and Eniwetok atolls, each consisting of chains of islands enclosing vast sheltered anchorages, and the former was attacked at the end of January 1944 under the code name Operation Flintlock. Once again, the Japanese defenders fought fanatically and when the Kwajalein Atoll was finally taken by 7 February less than 800 troops survived of the 8,675 who had occupied the islands at the start of the actions. However, heeding the lessons of Tarawa, the US Marines and Army lost only 372 men. Moving on, Eniwetok some 300 miles to the WNW was targeted under Operation Catchpole, but before that could happen the Japanese base at Truk, 600 miles away to the west, needed to be neutralised. Sometimes called the Gibraltar of the Pacific, this was a main base for the Japanese Combined Fleet. For these operations the newly formed Task Force 58 comprised no less than twelve carriers including four Essex class of which *Lexington* had been replaced by the newly arrived USS *Intrepid* (CV-11). Although the Japanese got wind of the impending attack and consequently withdrew many of the major naval units, the strikes on Truk (17–20 February) were

As the first Essex class carriers reached the Pacific Fleet in 1943, they were allocated to newly formed task forces which towards the end of the year began to conduct the first of a series of offensive operations. Initially these were against relatively unimportant targets which in effect provided the opportunity for the new air groups to gain their first taste of action. On 31 August 1943 Task Force 15, which comprised the USS *Essex* (CV-9) and *Yorktown* (CV-10) as well as the *USS Independence* (CVL-22), began a series of air strikes against Marcus Island, almost 2,000 miles west of Midway. This F6F Hellcat aboard *Yorktown* belongs to Lieutenant Commander J. Flatley, Commander CAG-5, as he prepares to lead the first strike. (NARA)

In September 1943 another early target was the island of Tarawa in the Gilbert Islands. Two months later this would be the objective of a full-scale amphibious assault but at this stage the raids were part of the softening up process and provided combat experience for the air groups. These were flown from the USS *Lexington* (CV-16) and two light fleet carriers, *Princeton* (CVL-23) and *Belleau Wood* (CVL-24). This image shows the Dauntless SBDs of VB-16 aboard *Lexington* after their return from strikes on 18 September 1943 during which two SBDs were lost to heavy AA fire, underlining that even these early familiarisation operations were still hazardous. (NARA)

outstandingly successful. Over 30 ships were sunk including many vital transports and over 300 aircraft destroyed in the air or on the ground. In the meantime, landings on the Eniwetok Atoll had also commenced on 17 February and were successfully completed by 24 February.

During the Truk raid *Intrepid* was hit by a torpedo launched from a lone Kate (naval Nakajima B5N torpedo bomber) in a night attack. This hit her stern, killing eleven men and jamming the rudder hard over. With some difficulty the ship reached Eniwetok for temporary repairs before sailing back to San Francisco for a comprehensive refit and was not fully operational until the following September. In the meantime, the remaining fast carriers of Task Force 58, under Admiral Mitscher, moved a further 1,000 miles to the west and on 23 February launched air strikes against the Mariana Islands, which included the large islands of Saipan and Guam.

In attacks on various airfields about 100 aircraft were destroyed on the ground and another 30 in aerial combats before the carriers withdrew and dispersed to replenish and make good their aircraft losses, which totalled about 80 from all the carriers involved. On the other hand, over 500 Japanese aircraft had been destroyed in these operations and more than 50 ships of various types sunk. In doing this the carrier task force had shown its ability to roam the Pacific at will and effectively defend itself from whatever attacks the Japanese were able to mount. It was a striking demonstration of US naval air power.

In fact, the Marianas were to be the next major objective. If they could be captured it would be a major breach in the Japanese outer defences and open the way for further assaults against the Philippines and, eventually, Japan itself. Possibly even more importantly from a strategic point of view, airfields on the islands would provide bases for the USAAF XXth Air Force and its growing fleet of B-29 Superfortress

A vital component of the carrier task forces was the fleet train which could refuel and resupply the carriers without them having to return to distant shore bases. This gave the task forces immense flexibility and allowed them to strike at widely separated targets within a relatively short timescale. Here the fleet tanker USS *Guadalupe* (AO-32) is photographed from the USS *Lexington* (CV-16) as oil fuel is passed through the suspended hose lines. On the tanker's starboard side the destroyer USS *Maury* (DD401) is also taking on fuel. (NARA)

bombers which would then be able to mount direct missions against targets in the Japanese homeland. Code-named Operation Forager, this involved landings on Saipan on 15 June 1944, and on Guam three days later. Cover for this operation was provided by the US Fifth Fleet and its Task Force 58 consisting of four carrier Task Groups which together included no less than six Essex class carriers (*Essex*, *Yorktown*, *Hornet*, *Bunker Hill*, *Wasp* and *Lexington*) and the *Enterprise* (CV-6), as well as ten Independence class light fleet carriers. In addition, several escort carriers (CVE) were available to provide reserve aircraft and to cover the actual landings. Even so, it took almost two months to defeat the Japanese garrisons on the Marianas, which also included Tinian and Rota.

The Imperial Japanese Navy and Army Air Forces had lost hundreds of valuable aircrew as well as aircraft as a result of the US Navy carrier strikes in late 1943 and early 1944. As a consequence, these forces remained relatively inactive for a while, but by June 1944 could muster nine aircraft carriers which together embarked about 450 aircraft. In addition, Admiral Ozawa, C-in-C First Mobile Fleet, could count on an additional 100 aircraft based ashore on the Marianas. However, the aircrew were mostly inexperienced and poorly trained when compared with their American counterparts. Nevertheless, Ozawa saw the invasion of the Marianas as a chance to precipitate a major engagement in which he hoped to inflict a serious defeat on the American fleet. The result was the Battle of the Philippine Sea which was fought over three days (19–21 June 1944) and ended in a decisive victory for the US Navy. In fact, it was the largest and most extensive carrier battle of the war and one after which the remaining Japanese carriers no longer constituted an effective fighting force. The Americans referred to the battle as the 'Great Marianas Turkey Shoot', a reflection of the fact that on 19 June alone the Japanese lost 346 aircraft out of a total of about 480 over the three days. In addition, three Japanese carriers were sunk including the *Taiho*, a brand-new 30,000-ton armoured aircraft carrier which had only commissioned two months earlier. US Navy losses in the battle totalled 130 aircraft from which at least 76 aircrew were rescued while no carriers were lost or even seriously damaged.

With the Marianas secured, the way was open for the invasion of the Philippines and further assaults on Iwo Jima and Okinawa. Although the Japanese carrier fleet had been neutralised, the IJN still possessed a powerful surface fleet and the objectives ahead would be defended with increased ferocity. In addition, a new and frightening form of warfare was about to be unleashed on the US carriers and many would sustain heavy damage and serious casualties as a result. Some of the hardest fighting was yet to come before victory could be secured.

In October 1943 the Fifth Fleet was reinforced by the arrival of another Essex class carrier, the USS *Bunker Hill* (CV-17), which in November took part in its first operation as part of TG 50.3 which also included *Essex* (CV-9) and *Independence* (CVL-22). These were involved in a series of strikes against Rabaul in the south-west Pacific in support of amphibious landings on Bougainville. At this stage there were four Essex class carriers operational with the fleet. (NARA)

As the Fifth Fleet grew in size, it was organised into Task Groups, each of which eventually comprised four carriers initially made up of two Essex class and two Independence class light fleet carriers (CVL). The latter carriers were quickly produced in 1942–3 by converting the hulls of Cleveland class cruisers then under construction. Although relatively small, they generally embarked around thirty-five aircraft and provided a welcome boost when they entered service in 1943. This is the lead ship of the class, USS *Independence* (CVL-22). (NARA)

44

Opposite above: By the beginning of November 1943 the US Pacific Fleet was able to deploy four Essex class carriers. While *Essex* and *Bunker Hill* covered landings at Bougainville in the Solomons, *Yorktown* and *Lexington*, together with the light carrier USS *Cowpens* (CVL-25) formed TG 50.1 to provide air cover for Operation Galvanic. *Yorktown* is seen here as viewed from the deck of *Lexington* on whose deck are ranged SBD Dauntless of VB-16. The Dauntless was a rugged dive bomber but aboard the Essex class carriers it was gradually replaced by the bigger and faster Curtiss SB2C Helldiver from late 1943 onwards. (NARA)

Opposite below: Another welcome reinforcement for the Fifth Fleet was the USS *Hornet* (CV-12), which joined Task Force 58 in the Marshall Islands on 20 March 1944. Subsequently she was involved in raids on the Palau Islands, attacked targets in New Guinea and took part in a heavy raid on the Japanese Fleet base at Truk. During Operation Forager she acted as flagship to TG 58.1 (Rear Admiral J.J. Cark USN) which also included the *Yorktown* (CV-10) and two light fleet carriers (*Bataan* and *Belleau Wood*). (NARA)

The occupation of the Marianas led to the last great carrier engagement of the Pacific War. While landing operations were supported by the escort carriers of Task Force 52, the threat of a massive attack by aircraft from the Japanese First Mobile Fleet was met by Task Force 58 which mustered no less than fifteen aircraft carriers including six Essex class. Here a Hellcat of VF-16 aboard the USS *Lexington* (CV-16) is preparing to depart for a strike against Saipan on 13 June 1944. In the background is the battleship USS *North Carolina* (BB-55) and, in the distance, two more carriers of TG 58.3. (NARA)

Above: For Operation Forager (the occupation of the Marianas) the carriers of Task Force 58 embarked no less than 468 Hellcats including two-dozen radar-equipped night-fighter variants. These Hellcats are part of *Lexington*'s air group which included thirty-eight day fighter Hellcats of VF-16 and four F6F-3N night fighters of VFN-76. In total the Fifth Fleet had over 1,200 aircraft embarked. Ranged against them, the First Mobile Fleet had 430 aircraft embarked but these were to be supplemented by several hundred aircraft of the 1st Air Fleet based on the Mariana airfields. (NARA)

Opposite above: On 19 June 1944 the USS *Bunker Hill* was part of TG 58.2 involved in Operation Forager. As part of the larger action which became the Battle of the Philippine Sea, *Bunker Hill* was attacked by a formation of D4Y (Judy) dive bombers escorted by a pair of Zero fighters. These were taken under fire by the ships of the task group including *Bunker Hill*'s 5in battery shown in this sequence of photographs. In the first the guns are at a low angle of elevation as they begin to engage the targets at long range. (NARA)

Opposite below: The guns now train aft at maximum elevation to track an approaching dive bomber while members of the crew, suddenly aware of the danger, rush for cover. (NARA)

47

While the guns continue to fire, a near miss bomb explodes in the water just off the ship's starboard side. During this attack the combined fire of the task group ships accounted for five aircraft. (NARA)

The Grumman TBF Avenger torpedo bomber had an inauspicious start to its career when VT-8, the first squadron to receive the aircraft, lost five out of six committed in the Battle of Midway on 1 June 1942. However, in carrier operations in 1943 the Avenger proved to be a tough and adaptable aircraft and subsequently most Essex class carriers embarked a squadron of sixteen to twenty Avengers as part of their air groups right to the end of the war. However, Grumman was heavily involved in the production of Hellcat fighters and subcontracted Avenger construction to the Eastern Aircraft Division of General Motors which produced 7,546 Avengers (designated TBM) compared with 2,290 built as TBFs by Grumman. (NARA)

Chapter Four

Aboard the Essex Class

An aircraft carrier is probably the most complex war machine ever to enter combat. At the time of their construction the Essex class were among the most advanced in the world and certainly the most efficient when it came to embarking and operating aircraft. Although designed to accommodate 90 aircraft, it was not uncommon for over 100 to be embarked and the normal complement of about 2,600 men increased to 3,500 when the air group with its aircrew, operations staff, aircraft handlers, engineers and maintainers was embarked. This placed an enormous strain on the ship as all these sailors and airmen had to be accommodated and fed. In addition, the aircraft required large quantities of highly inflammable aviation fuel which had to be stored under special arrangements, as well as supplies of bombs, rockets, torpedoes and ammunition. As far as the ship was concerned, it was run by the command team under the captain with individual senior officers responsible for the various departments including gunnery, radar and electronics, communications, engineering, supply and catering, and medical.

When a carrier first commissioned it was likely that as many as three-quarters of the crew would be going to sea for the first time, having just completed their training. This was especially the case as the war progressed and the numerous shore-based training establishments produced ever increasing numbers of sailors trained in various specialities to form the crews of the new ships, which were being built in large numbers. Consequently, it would take several months for the ship to work up to full operational efficiency before it could join the active fleet. In this time the crew could become familiar with the complex layout of the ship and, as well as becoming proficient at their own specialisation, be able to assist in other tasks (such as damage control) when required. Having brought the ship to an acceptable state of preparedness, the air group could then be embarked, which required a further period of training so that the various squadrons could learn to work together, new pilots could build up experience and the flight-deck crews get used to handling the aircraft on a busy and crowded flight deck. All this training was known as 'working up' and was usually conducted in the Caribbean area, generally safe from enemy activity and where weather conditions would not hinder progress. This working up process generally occupied five or six months after the ship had officially commissioned.

The following images show some of the activities aboard an Essex class aircraft carrier as well as detailed views of some of the ship's armament, equipment and aircraft.

The Essex class carriers were equipped with a battery of effective heavy AA guns in the shape of twelve 5in/38cal guns. Eight of these were carried in four twin mountings, two in front of the island superstructure, as shown in this view aboard the USS *Randolph* (CV-15), and another pair aft of the island. The remaining four guns were arranged in single mountings along the port-side edge of the flight deck. The 5in/38cal gun was a standard weapon in the US Navy and in addition to the Essex class and other carriers, it was the secondary armament on battleships and cruisers and the main armament of almost all the destroyers. (NARA)

Empty 5in shell cases being collected and stowed after a practice firing detail aboard USS *Franklin* (CV-13) in March 1945. (NARA)

The fire of the 5in guns was controlled from two Mk.37 gunnery directors mounted on the island superstructure. These measured or estimated the range, bearing, height, course and speed of the target and this information was fed into the analogue fire-control computers shown here in the Central Fire Control Room (CFCR) aboard USS *Yorktown* (CV-10). These in turn signalled instructions to the guns in terms of elevation and bearing and to their adjacent fuze-setting machines. Shell-burst position or fall of shot observed from the director would be transmitted to the CFCR so that relevant corrections to improve accuracy could be made. (NARA)

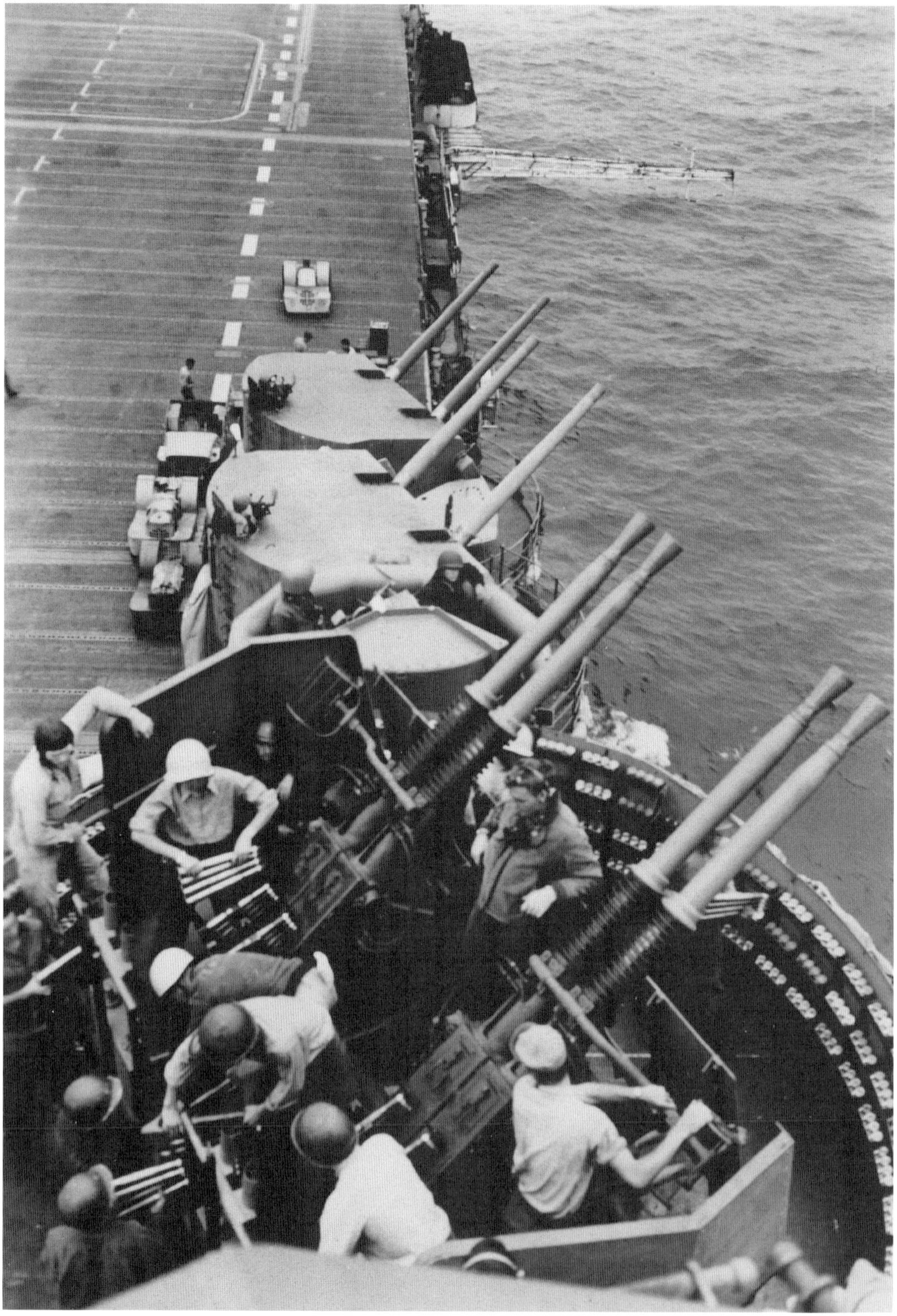

Above: The light AA armament also included dozens of single 20mm guns, six of which are here mounted in a gallery on the forward port side of the flight deck. This photo showing gunners carrying out a practice firing was taken on 11 December 1944 aboard the USS *Wasp* (CV-18) as she formed part of TG 38.1 moving to support landings at Luzon and Mindoro in the Philippines. In the background is sister ship USS *Yorktown* (CV-10). (NARA)

Opposite: The standard close-range AA gun was the Bofors 40mm in quadruple mountings such as this one aboard the USS *Hornet* (CV-12). As originally completed, the early Essex class carried eight 40mm quad mounts, four on the island superstructure, two on the port-side deck edge adjacent to the single 5in/38cal guns, and one each at the bow and stern. As the war progressed these numbers were boosted so that by August 1945 most operational ships carried seventeen or eighteen quad mounts for a total of sixty-eight or seventy-two 40mm guns supplemented by up to sixty 20mm guns. (NARA)

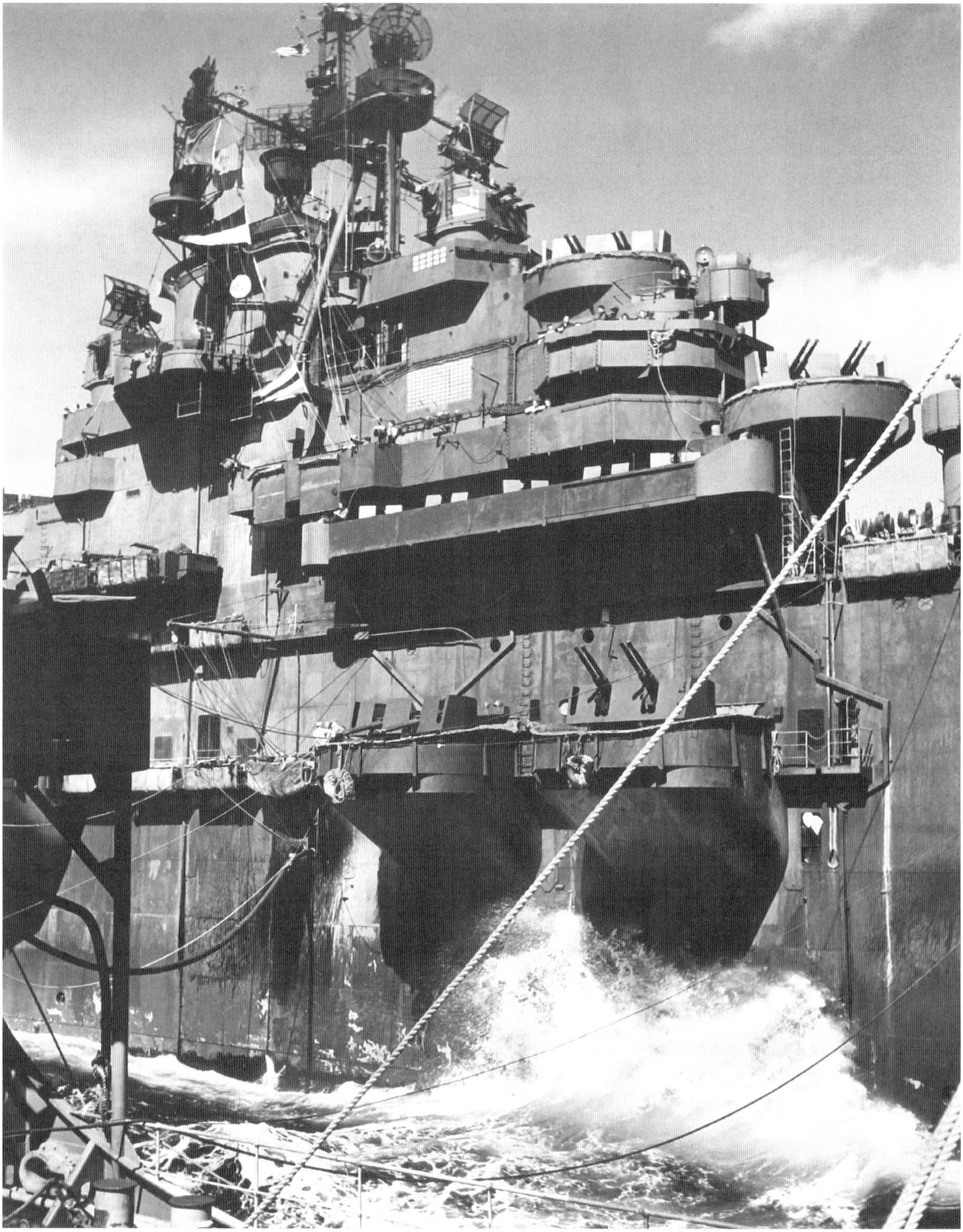

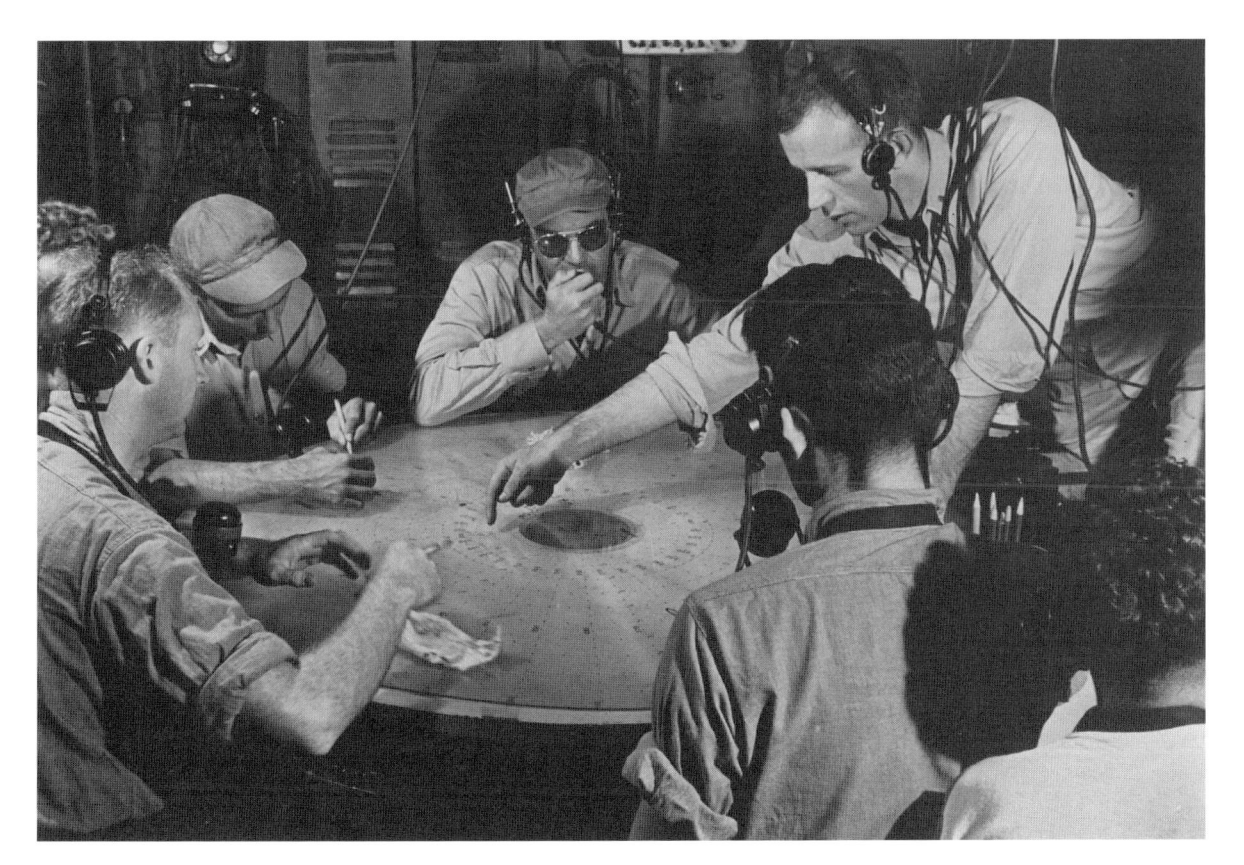

Above: The fighter plot aboard USS *Lexington* (CV-16), January 1945. The team sitting around the circular plotting table annotate information received through their headphones from various radar operators to build up a picture of the air situation. The fighter controller (centre) is in direct contact with the fighters in the air and can direct them to intercept incoming raids. Throughout the war this system was constantly improved and evolved, although initially the USN relied heavily on earlier RN experience gained in 1940–1 and USN observers who had studied the RAF's air defence system during the Battle of Britain. (NARA)

Opposite: This close-up view of USS *Yorktown* (CV-10) was taken as the ship conducted a Replenishment at Sea (RAS) while operating in the South China Sea in January 1945 and gives a good impression of the sheer size of these ships. Of particular interest are the two quadruple 40mm AA mountings carried on sponsons on the side of the hull. These had been fitted in the previous September and brought the total of such mountings to eighteen. In addition, she carried sixty-one single 20mm guns, five of which can be seen in the gallery at the base of the island. Each quad 40mm required at least eleven men (sometimes more with additional ammunition handlers) to maintain a high rate of fire which meant that these guns alone required around 750 men when the ship was in action. (NARA)

By 1945 US Navy capital ships carried a bewildering array of electronic equipment as illustrated in this view showing the foremast of USS *Hornet* (CV-12). The larger circular antenna is for a newly fitted SP aircraft direction radar with a Type BO rectangular mesh IFF antenna mounted on top. The large 'bedstead' antenna behind the pole mast is for the SK long-range air search radar while the small parabolic antenna on the platform at the top of the pole mast is an SG short-range radar mainly used for navigation. The curved aerial at the very top of the pole mast extension is for the YE aircraft homing beacon while at lower left is one of the Mk.37 directors for the 5in guns which carries a Mk.4 fire-control radar antenna. (NARA)

Opposite above: Although the ship carried a substantial outfit of AA guns, the first line of defence rested with the fighter squadrons embarked on the various carriers. From the time the first Essex class commissioned until early 1945 these were almost exclusively Grumman F6F Hellcats. These examples preparing to fly off from USS *Hornet* (CV-12) in May 1945 belong to VF-17 and bear the white tail markings of the ship's Air Group 17 (CAG-17). (NARA)

Opposite below: In the closing stages of the Pacific War the Vought F4U Corsair finally began to supplement or replace the Hellcat aboard some of the Essex class carriers. Although it had entered service early in 1943, it had initially been allocated to land-based squadrons and was only cleared for carrier operations in April 1944. The Corsair was considerably faster than the Hellcat (425mph against 386mph) and eventually its pilots claimed 2,140 Japanese aircraft destroyed for the loss of only 189 Corsairs. This F4U-1D Corsair belongs to VF-5 aboard USS *Franklin* (CV-13) in March 1945 where they had replaced the Hellcats of VF-13. (NARA)

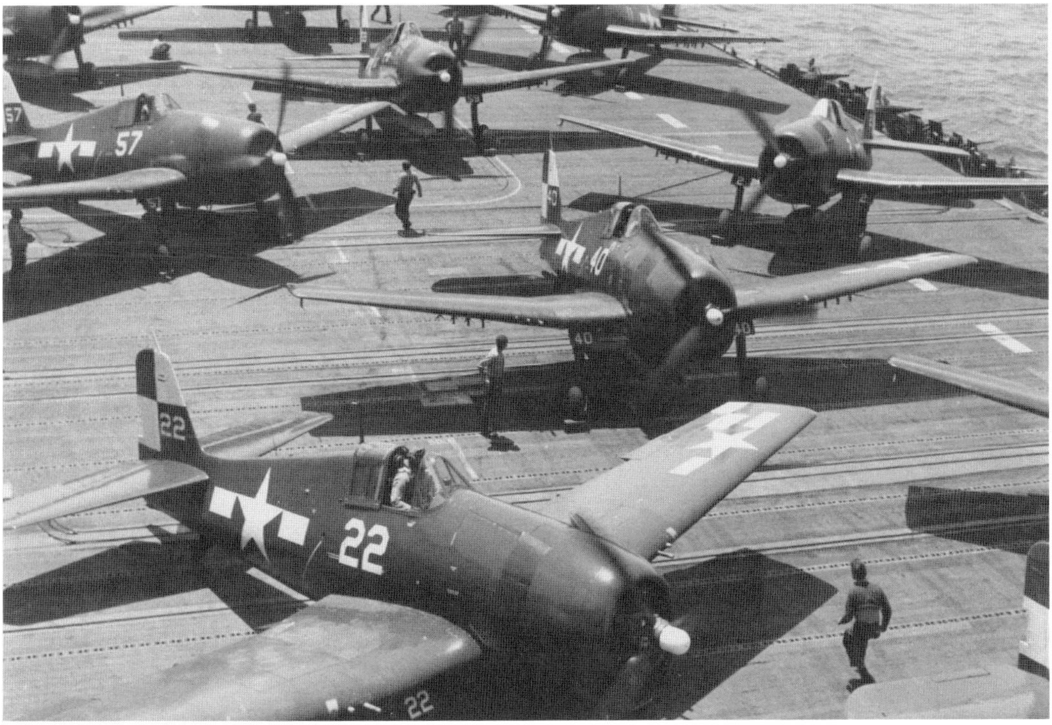
57
40
22
22

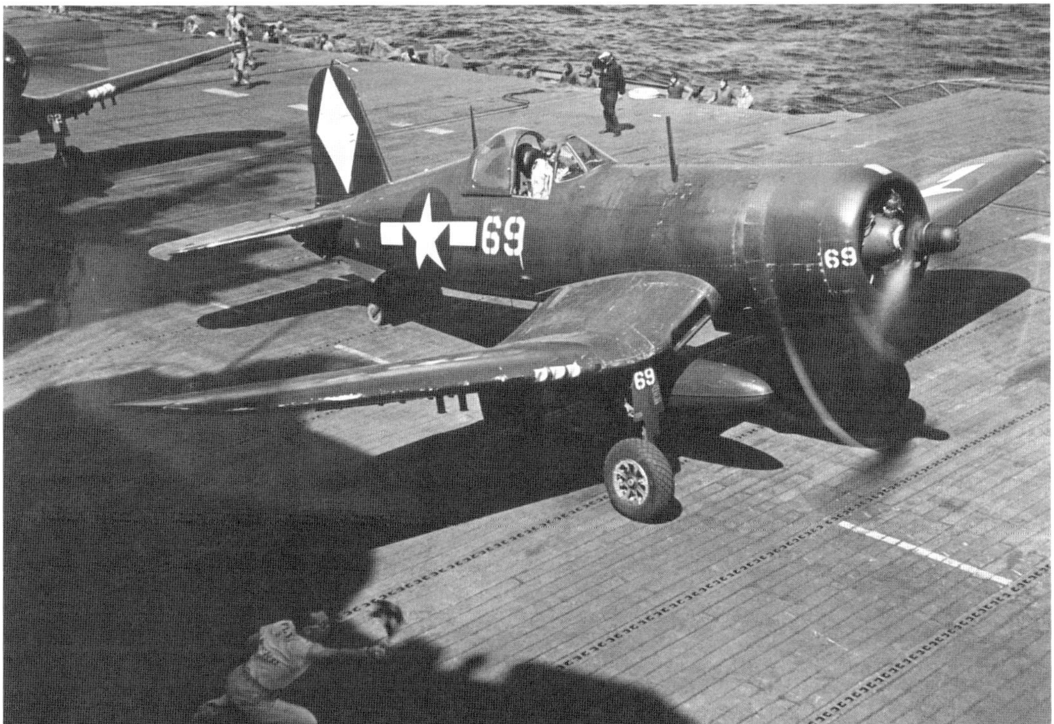
69
69
69

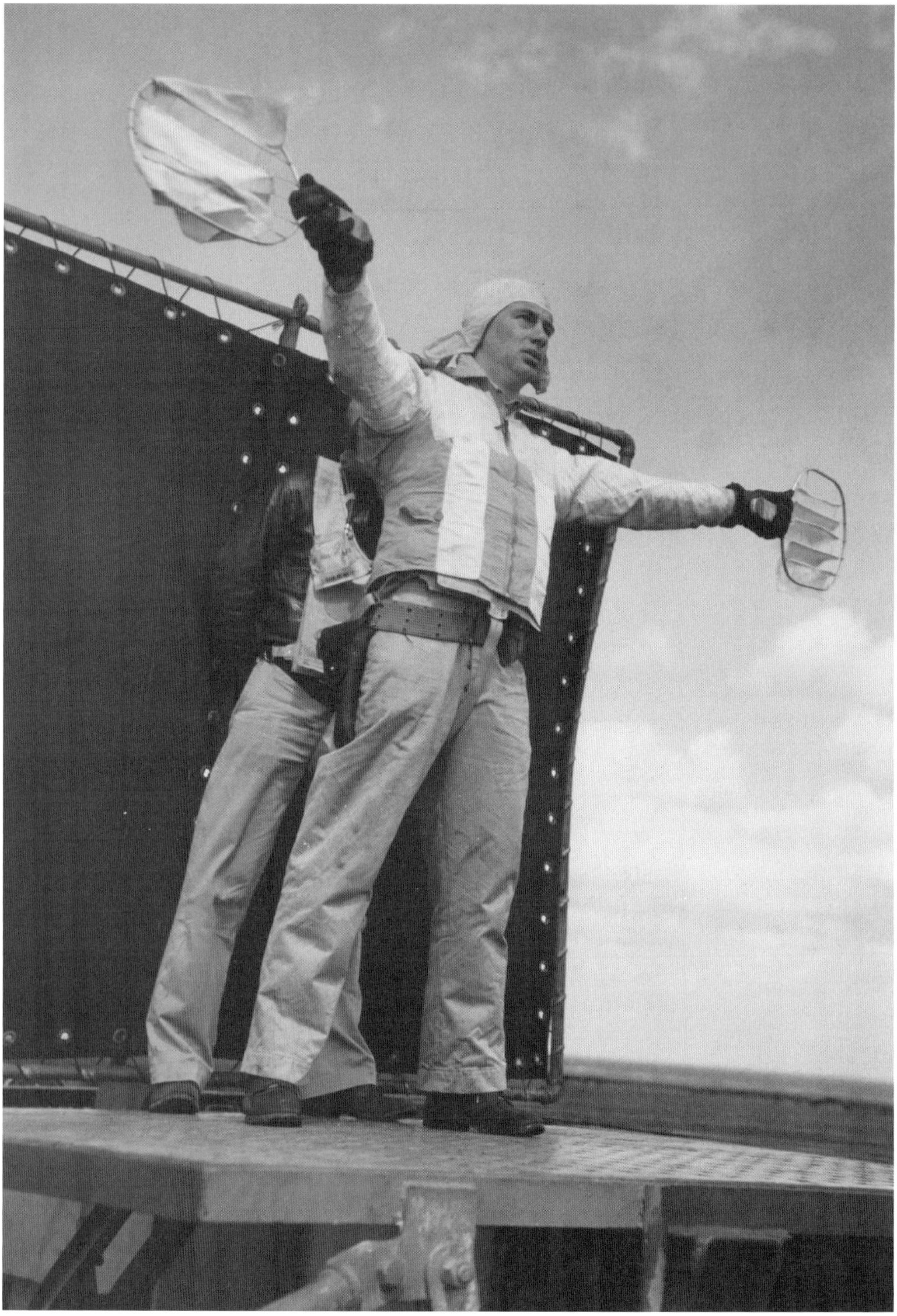

Opposite: An important member of the air group team was the Landing Deck Officer (LDO). He was always an experienced pilot trained to guide pilots into a successful landing by means of signals conveyed by the two bats. These and the LDO's jacket were white or brightly coloured so that the movement of the bats could be seen against the dark screen behind. The LDO's signals were mandatory and had to be obeyed by the pilot – in contrast to RN procedures where the signals were regarded as for guidance only. This differing philosophy initially caused some confusion when RN and USN aircraft occasionally operated from each other's carriers. The LDO shown here is aboard the USS *Hancock* (CV-19) which had joined the US Third Fleet in the Pacific in July 1944. (NARA)

Even with assistance from the LDO, landing accidents were not uncommon. In this case a Hellcat of VF-17 landing aboard the USS *Hornet* (CV-12) has missed all eight arrester wires and has run into the crash barrier erected abreast the island to prevent such events resulting in an aircraft running into others parked on the forward section of the flight deck. The Hellcat is now being disentangled from the barrier, which has been lowered, before being moved forward to clear the deck for the next landing aircraft. Apart from the twisted propeller, it doesn't appear to be too badly damaged and will be repaired using the onboard facilities. (NARA)

The first eight Essex class incorporated a catapult to launch aircraft from the hangar deck but this was deleted in later ships. It was rarely used in practice, although here its use is demonstrated by the launch of a Hellcat from the USS *Hornet* (CV-12). (NMNA)

Although the fighters were vital for defence of the ship and its associated task force, the power of an aircraft carrier lay in its squadrons of torpedo and dive bombers. The Grumman TBF Avenger torpedo bomber (which was also produced in large numbers by the Eastern Aircraft Division of General Motors as the TBM) first entered service in 1942 and subsequently equipped all VT squadrons aboard the Essex class carriers from mid-1943 onwards. A unique feature of this aircraft was that its load of bombs or a torpedo could be carried in an internal bomb bay, thus reducing drag and improving performance. A total of 9,836 were produced and the type remained in service in the post-war era, mainly as an anti-submarine aircraft until 1954. (NARA)

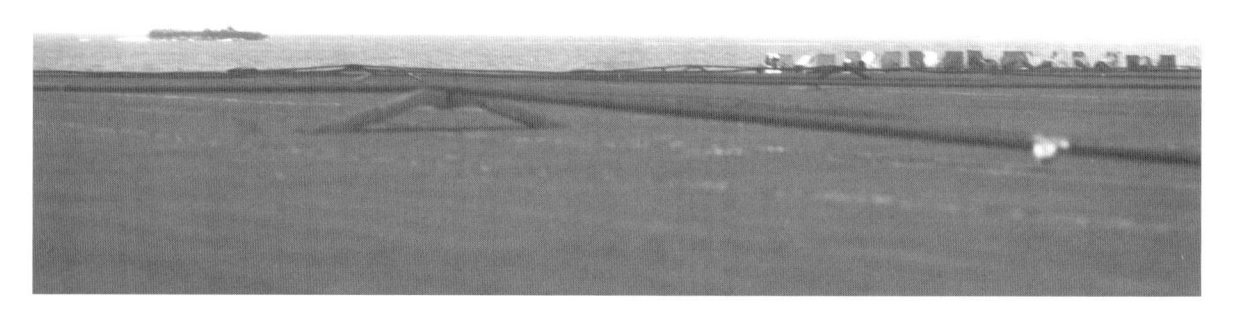

Above: Although the Curtiss SB2C Helldiver prototype flew in December 1940, it did not become fully operational until November 1943 due to significant problems during its development. Even in its final form it was disliked by its pilots on account of poor handling characteristics as well as various equipment deficiencies. Nevertheless, by 1945 it had almost completely replaced the much-liked SDB Dauntless in the fleet's VB squadrons. This SB2C-1C Helldiver landing aboard USS *Essex* (CV-9) in October 1944 belongs to Bombing Squadron 15 (VB-15) which at that time had a strength of twenty-five aircraft. (NMNA)

Opposite: One feature on the Essex class carriers was the introduction of a deck-edge lift to supplement the two situated fore and aft on the centreline of the flight deck. This proved very useful for a number of purposes apart from transferring aircraft between the hangar and the flight deck. Here a mix of 500 and 1,000lb bombs are being prepared to arm a strike by Helldivers of VB-15 against targets on Guam during Operation Forager, June 1944. (NARA)

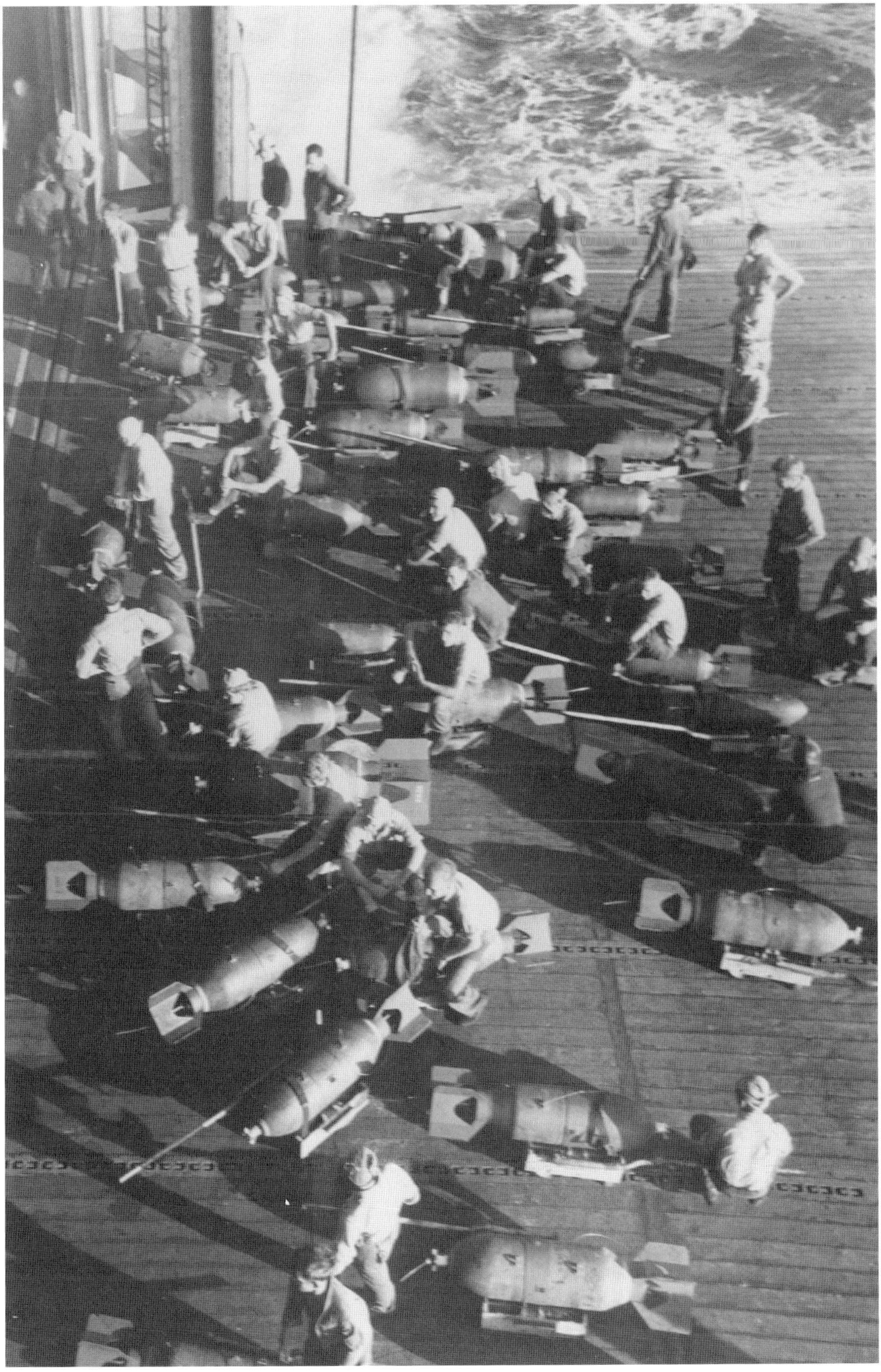

64

Above: Damage control was a vital function of the ship's organisation. Several of the Essex class were severely damaged by air and kamikaze attacks but were saved by the prompt actions of their crews. There were at least two main damage-control stations so that if one was put out of action the other could co-ordinate efforts to save the ship. This one is aboard USS *Lexington* (CV-16) and shows the damage-control team surrounded by charts and diagrams detailing the layout of the ship and its various systems. Note the sound-powered telephones by which they could communicate with and direct the groups of sailors fighting fires, flooding and other damage. (NARA)

Opposite above: In the aircraft control room aboard USS *Randolph* (CV-15) an officer and mechanic maintain a record of the constantly changing status of every aircraft on board. (NARA)

Opposite below: Communications were another vital element of the operation of the ship. Here the 'radio gang' aboard USS *Hornet* (CV-12) operate some of the various radio sets which enabled communication with other ships and the task-force commanders, as well as the all-important radio links to the aircraft. In addition, long-range HF sets allowed communication with various fleet commands ashore at Pearl Harbor and other bases including those on the US west coast. (NARA)

A view of the hangar deck aboard USS *Yorktown* (CV-10) in 1943 during the ship's first year of operations. In the foreground between rows of Hellcat fighters ordnance specialists work on assembling bombs while in the background a section of the crew watch a movie projected on a screen suspended from the hangar roof. At the back of the hangar can be seen a Dauntless dive bomber and several more Hellcats. (NARA)

An aircraft carrier was a totally self-dependent community of over 3,000 men who had to be organised, accommodated, fed and clothed. In support, complete medical and dental health facilities were provided including operating theatres such as this one aboard the USS *Randolph* where a surgeon and anaesthetist (both US Navy Reserve officers), supported by two Pharmacist's Mates, carry out an emergency hernia operation in May 1945. (NARA)

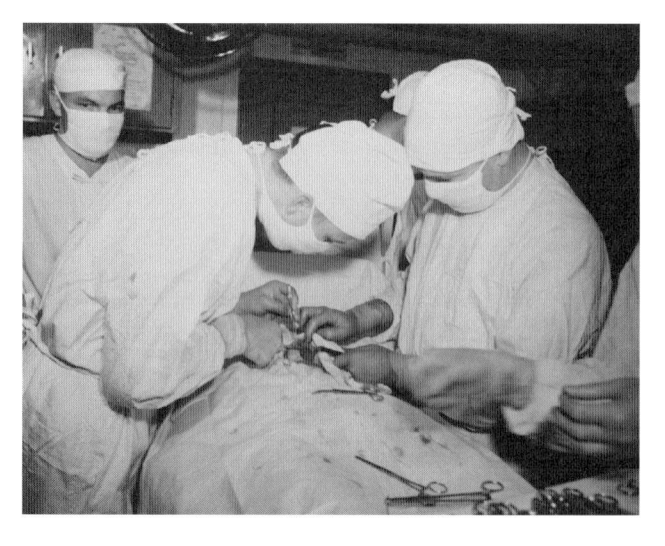

The majority of the men aboard an Essex class carrier in the Second World War were accommodated in crowded mess decks similar to this one in USS *Yorktown*. Maximum utilisation of space is achieved by having three layers of bunks, all of which could fold away when not in use. Although there was forced air ventilation, there was no air conditioning, and in tropical waters conditions could be very uncomfortable. (NARA)

Chapter Five

Through Kamikaze to Victory

By late 1944 the Pacific Fleet had fought its way across the Pacific to the point where it could direct its forces (which now included eight Essex class carriers) to the liberation of the Philippines in October 1944 and then the occupation of Iwo Jima (Operation Detachment, February 1945) and Okinawa (Operation Iceberg, April 1945), which were stepping stones to the final assault on the Japanese mainland islands. The landing of US forces on the Philippines prompted a series of naval engagements which made up the Battle of Leyte Gulf, the greatest naval battle ever fought and one that put an end to the Imperial Japanese Navy as an effective fighting force. However, all these landings were vigorously opposed and the casualties on both sides were of a very high order. This was particularly the case for the Japanese defenders who fought with fanatical determination, often literally to the last man.

At sea the supporting naval forces came under a frightening new form of aerial attack – kamikaze suicide strikes. Inevitably the prime targets for these attacks were the aircraft carriers and in the course of the various campaigns no less than eight Essex class were hit at one time or another. In some cases the ships were able to quickly repair the damage and continue in action but more often they would have to be withdrawn for repairs, although every attack resulted in a grievous loss of life. In 1944 the Pacific Fleet had occupied the enormous atoll at Ulithi, which provided a large natural harbour where repair and maintenance facilities were set up. The carriers and other ships of the task forces would regularly return there between operations.

In 1943 Admiral Chester Nimitz USN was the C-in-C Pacific Fleet which included the Third Fleet Under Admiral William (Bill) Halsey USN, operating in the South-West Pacific and supporting advances in the Solomon Islands and New Guinea, and the Fifth Fleet based at Pearl Harbor commanded by Admiral Raymond Spruance USN. In 1944, as US forces converged on the Philippines, these two fleets were effectively combined and the Fast Carrier Force, Pacific, was designated as Task Force 58 under the command of the then Rear Admiral

Fleet Admiral Chester W. Nimitz USN, C-in-C Pacific Fleet, (right) with Admiral Raymond Spruance USN commanding US Navy Fifth Fleet. (NARA)

Admiral William F. Halsey USN, Commander US Navy Third Fleet. (NARA)

Admiral Marc Mitscher USN, Commander Fast Carrier Task Forces. (NARA)

Marc Mitscher (later full Admiral). An arrangement came into place whereby command of the combined fleets and the carrier task force would alternate between Spruance and Halsey and would be designated Third Fleet/Task Force 38 or Fifth Fleet/Task Force 58 depending on who was in command. This system allowed one admiral and his staff to be planning the next operation while the other conducted a current operation. Thus, for example, the occupation of the Marianas (Operation Forager) had been supported by Task Force 58 under Spruance while Halsey's Task Force 38 covered the occupation of the Philippines and the Leyte Gulf battles. Iwo Jima and Okinawa again saw Spruance commanding Task Force 58 until 28 May 1945 when command devolved to Halsey and Task Force 38, which was then responsible for the final operations off Japan. The Essex class carriers were at the centre of all these actions and by March 1945, just before Operation Iceberg (Okinawa), there were no less than nine available supported by five Independence class light fleet carriers as well as the veteran *Enterprise* (CV-6). Had Operation Olympic (the invasion of Kyushu) planned for November

1945 gone ahead it would have included thirteen Essex class with three more available as replacements or reinforcements by the end of the year.

These operations are covered in this chapter, which includes many dramatic images showing the impact and aftermath of both kamikaze and conventional attacks as well as the equally damaging effects of a series of typhoons which hit the fleets during the summer of 1945.

Forming part of TG 38.4, USS *Franklin* (CV-13) played an active part in the Leyte Gulf actions and her aircraft assisted in the sinking of the battleship *Musashi* and the subsequent attacks on the Japanese carriers off Cape Engaño. After these naval actions Task Force 38 remained on station to support land operations ashore. This prompted a fierce response from Japanese shore-based aircraft and on 30 October 1944 kamikazes successfully crashed into the *Franklin*, *Intrepid* (CV-11) and *Belleau Wood* (CVL-24), which all had to return to Ulithi for temporary repairs. This image shows the immediate aftermath of this attack with *Franklin* on fire in the foreground and the similarly afflicted *Belleau Wood* in the background. (NHHC)

Above: In the actions around Leyte Gulf (24–6 October 1944) the USS *Lexington* (CV-16) played a prominent part. Her aircraft were involved in the sinking of the battleship *Musashi* and the aircraft carriers *Chitose* and *Zuiho*, while her aircraft alone were responsible for sinking the carrier *Zuikaku* (the last survivor of the six carriers that had launched the infamous attack on Pearl Harbor) and the heavy cruiser *Nachi*. Retribution followed in the form of a kamikaze attack on 5 November and this photo shows the aircraft in its final dive towards the ship. It subsequently hit the island superstructure causing considerable damage, but the fires were quickly brought under control and the ship remained in action and able to operate aircraft less than 30 minutes later. (NARA)

Opposite above: In late November 1944 Task Force 38 was still engaged in support of US forces fighting ashore to secure the Philippines. On 25 November 1944 the USS *Essex* was hit by a kamikaze which struck the flight deck amidships – the favourite aiming point for such attacks. In fact, it hit the port edge of the flight deck causing damage to the ship which was relatively easy to repair, but destroyed several aircraft parked there and killed fifteen men and injured forty-four others. Repairs were quickly effected at Ulithi and the ship was back in action less than three weeks later. (NARA)

Opposite below: A spectacular shot showing the kamikaze flown by Lieutenant Yamaguchi about to hit the USS *Essex*. The aircraft is a Yokosuka D4Y-3 Suisei (Comet), a high-speed naval dive bomber of which this radial engined version entered service in 1944. In fact, a subsequent version, the D4Y-4, was later produced in 1945 and was specifically modified for the kamikaze mission as a single-seater armed with a single 800kg bomb semi-recessed under the fuselage and fitted with three auxiliary rockets which could be used to boost take-off performance or increase speed in the final attack phase. (NARA)

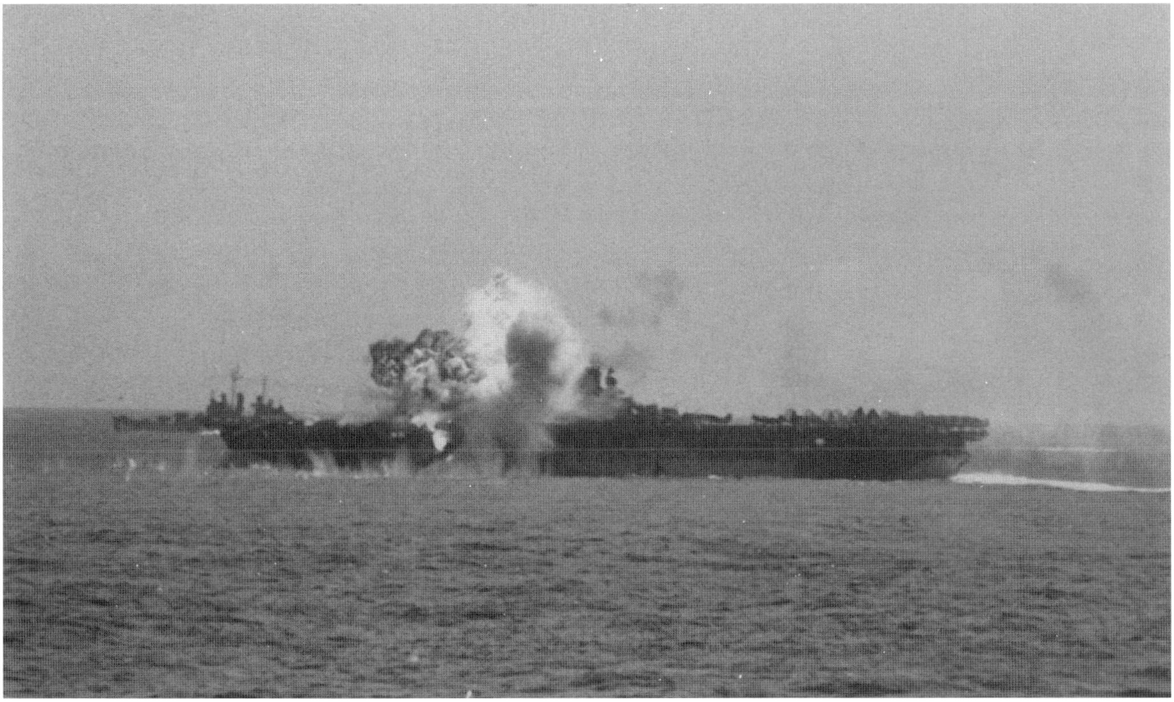

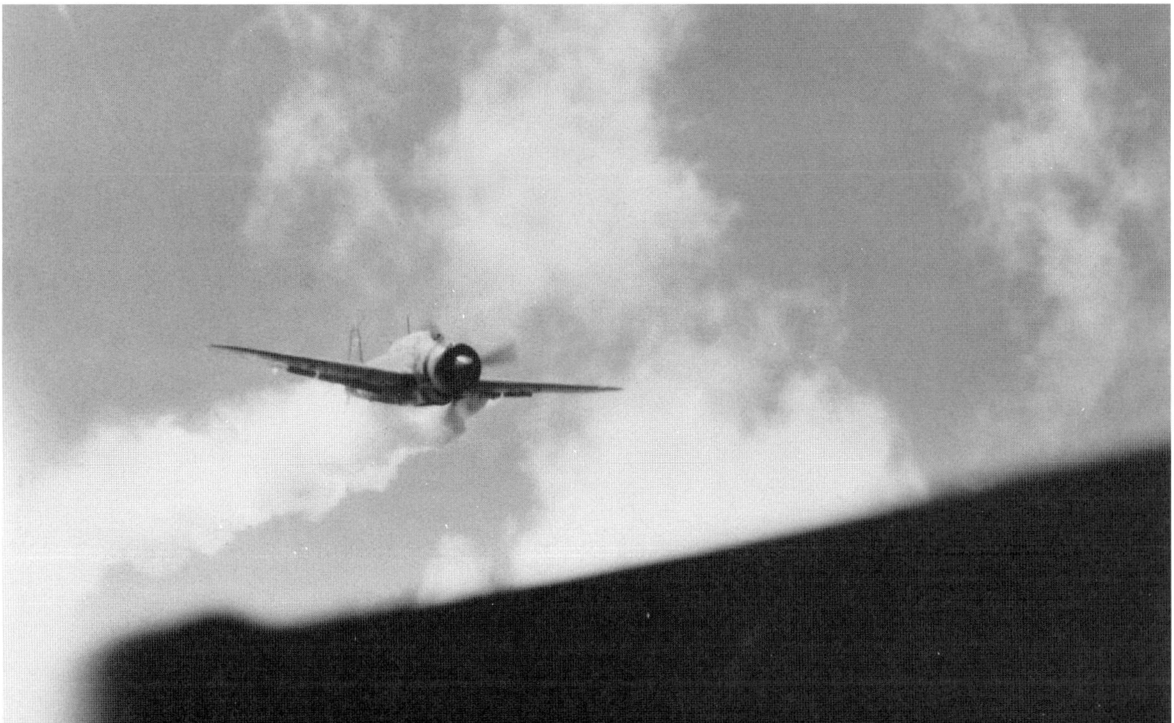

Above: The increasing number of Essex class carriers available for action in the Pacific by the end of 1944 is well illustrated by this view of the Ulithi anchorage on 2 December 1944. At anchor, from left to right, are the USS *Wasp* (CV-18), USS *Yorktown* (CV-10), USS *Hornet* (CV-12), USS *Hancock* (CV-19), while in the foreground are Hellcat fighters of VF-80 aboard USS *Ticonderoga* (CV-14). Not in the picture but also forming part of the Third Fleet were USS *Essex* (CV-9) and USS *Lexington* (CV-15). In commission but undergoing a refit was USS *Bunker Hill* (CV-17), while USS *Franklin* (CV-13) was also in a US port undergoing repairs following a kamikaze strike. (NARA)

Opposite above: In December 1944 the carriers of Task Force 38 supported landings by US forces at Lingayen Gulf on Luzon, the most northerly of the Philippines. In these operations 170 Japanese aircraft were claimed as destroyed against a loss in combat of 27 US aircraft, although a further 38 were lost in accidents. Bad weather including a typhoon in the area caused further operations to be abandoned and the task force returned to Ulithi. This view looking aft from USS *Hancock* (CV-19) shows ships of TG 38.2 as they approach the anchorage on 22 December 1944, USS *Independence* (CVL-22) astern followed by the USS *Hornet* (CV-12). (NARA)

Opposite below: The damage caused by the kamikaze strike on 30 October 1944 resulted in the USS *Franklin* returning stateside for repairs and she did not rejoin the Pacific Fleet via Pearl Harbor until early March 1945. Only a few days later, on 19 March, she was part of TG 58.2 launching strikes against the Japanese mainland in support of operations against Okinawa when she was hit by two 250kg bombs from a single dive bomber. One struck amidships and penetrated the hangar deck, while the other hit aft and also penetrated through two decks before exploding. The resulting fires quickly spread and engulfed the ship. (NARA)

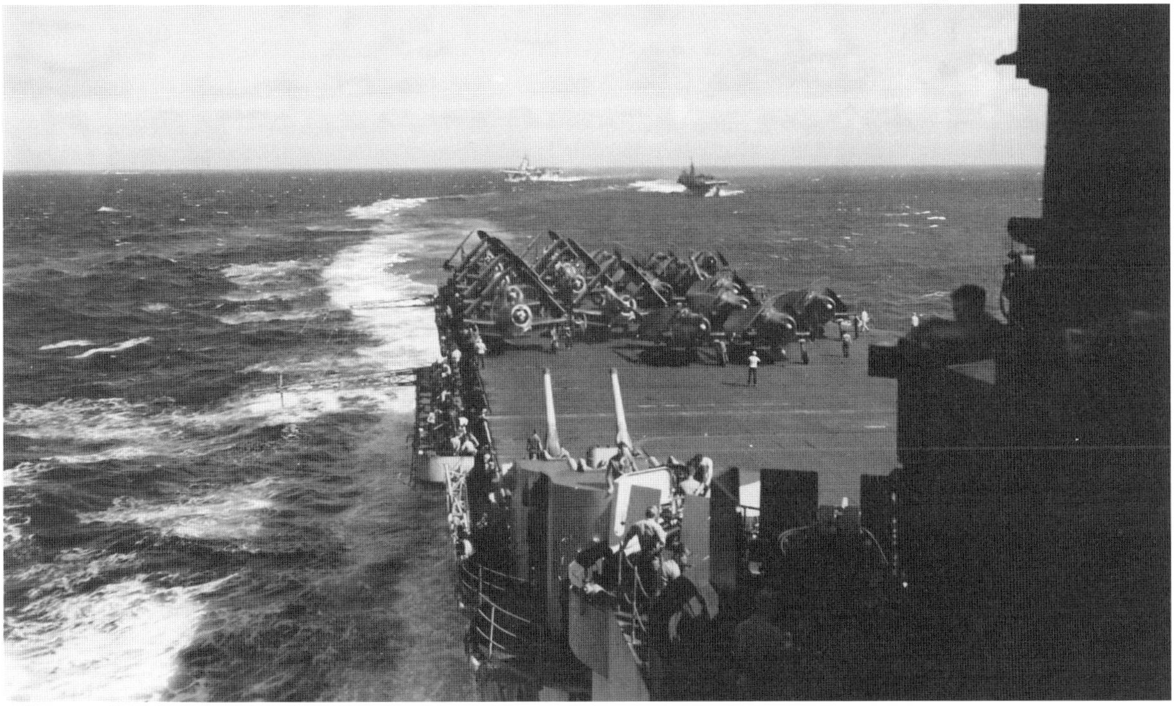

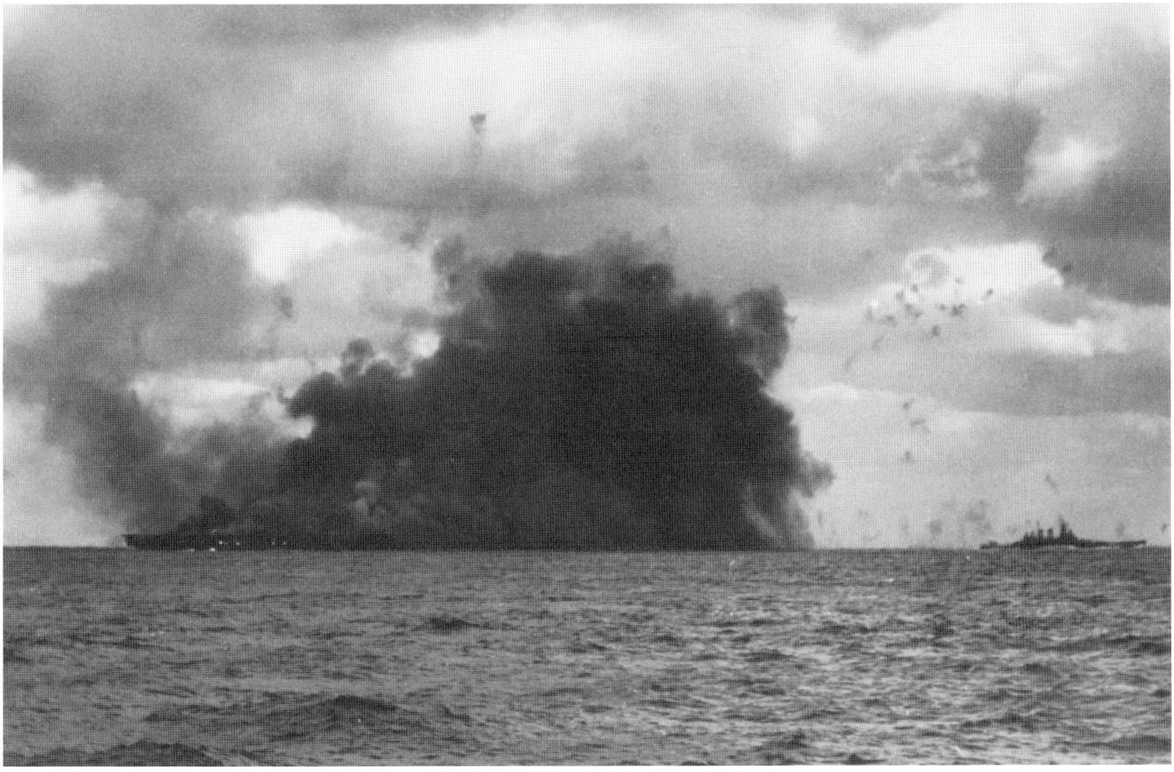

76

Opposite above: At the time of the attack, the *Franklin* had fully fuelled and armed aircraft on deck and others in a similar state in the hangar. The exploding bombs set these on fire and caused the ordnance to explode. Gasoline vapour from fractured fuel lines ignited in a massive explosion which swept through the hangar deck. The intensity and ferocity of the fire buckled the after flight deck and caused extensive damage, as can be seen in this dramatic image taken from the cruiser USS *Santa Fe* (CL-60), which came to assist and evacuate survivors. (NARA)

Opposite below: With the after section of the carrier enveloped in thick smoke, the *Santa Fe* came alongside on the starboard bow to take off numerous wounded and casualties as well as non-essential crew and members of the embarked air group. However, several hundred men remained on board, determined to save the ship and many can be seen gathered on the relative safety of the forward flight deck. (NARA)

Although still wreathed in smoke, by the time this photo was taken the fires were coming under control and the cruiser USS *Pittsburgh* is manoeuvring in preparation to take the *Franklin* under tow. Wartime modifications including extra armament and a strengthened flight deck had increased displacement and reduced stability margins which became critical when the thousands of gallons of water used to fight the fires were added. As a result, the ship developed a substantial list to starboard and at one stage there was a serious risk of it capsizing. (NARA)

Above: Eventually, after several hours, the fires were extinguished, and stability restored as the water was pumped out. Initially she was towed out of danger by the *Pittsburgh* but remarkably the *Franklin*'s crew were eventually able to raise steam and enabled the ship to get underway on her own power. After temporary repairs at Ulithi and Pearl Harbor, she reached the Brooklyn Naval Yard, New York, on 28 April 1945. This photo shows the mangled state of the flight deck at that time. The *Franklin* incident was a major tragedy for the US Navy – no less than 807 sailors were killed and at least 487 wounded. These figures were the highest experienced by any ship that survived an attack and were exceeded only by the 1,177 killed aboard the battleship USS *Arizona* (BB-39) sunk at Pearl Harbor in December 1941. (NHHC)

Opposite above: In January 1945 the carriers of Task Force 38 deployed into the South China Sea and successfully attacked Japanese shipping and other targets as far east and south as Hong Kong and Saigon – an amazing demonstration of the flexibility of this form of warfare. This formation of TBM Avengers belonging to VT-4 aboard USS *Essex* (CV-9) is en route to a strike against Japanese installations on the Chinese mainland. (NHHC)

Opposite below: On 21 January as Task Force 38 returned northwards a series of strikes were mounted against Formosa and adjacent islands which in turn prompted ferocious kamikaze attacks. These concentrated on the carrier USS *Ticonderoga* (CV-14), which suffered a hit on the flight deck just forward of the island. More kamikazes mounted another attack and although three were shot down, a fourth hit the starboard side causing fires and over 100 casualties. This photo was taken from USS *Essex* (CV-9) and the burning *Ticonderoga* can be seen in the background. (NARA)

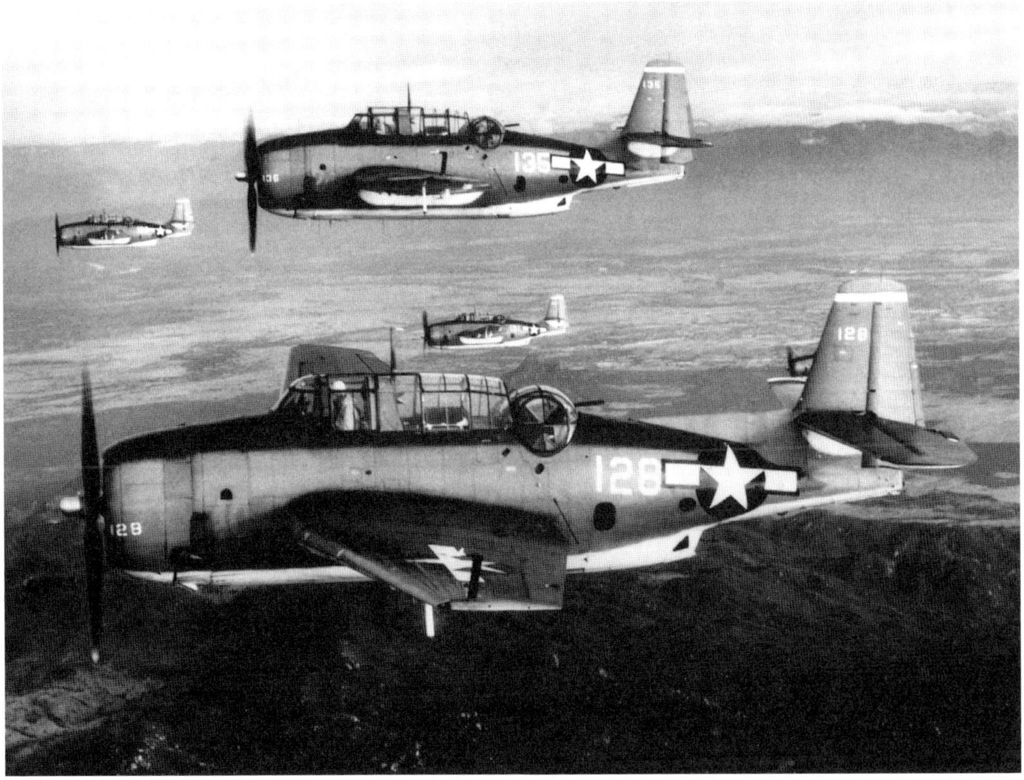
135
128

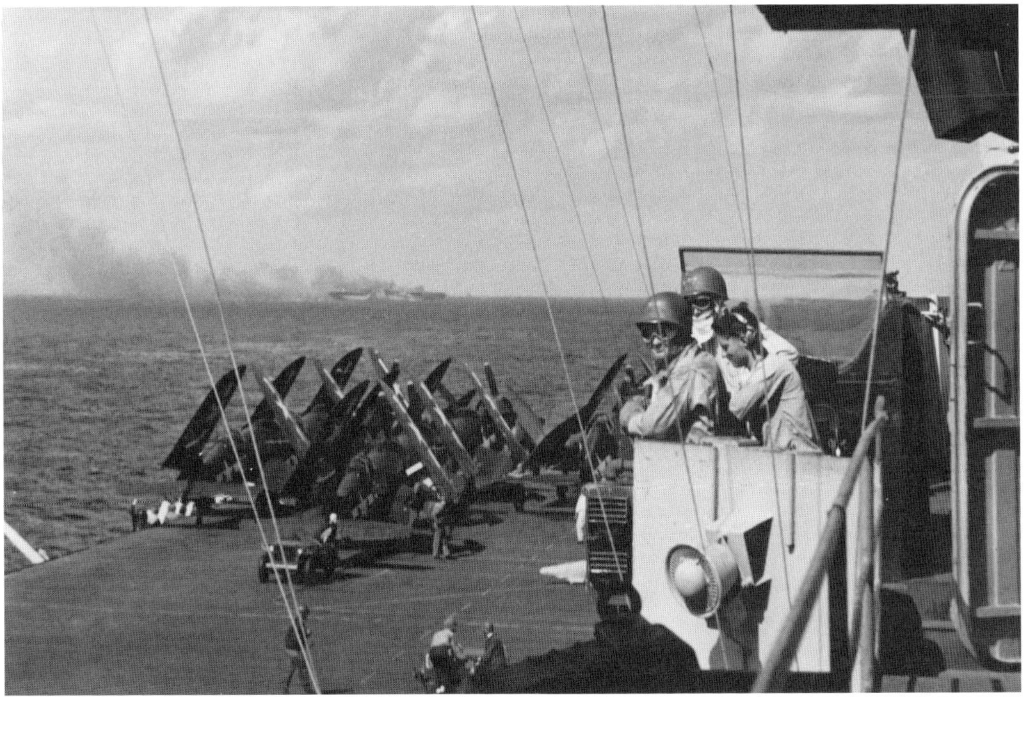

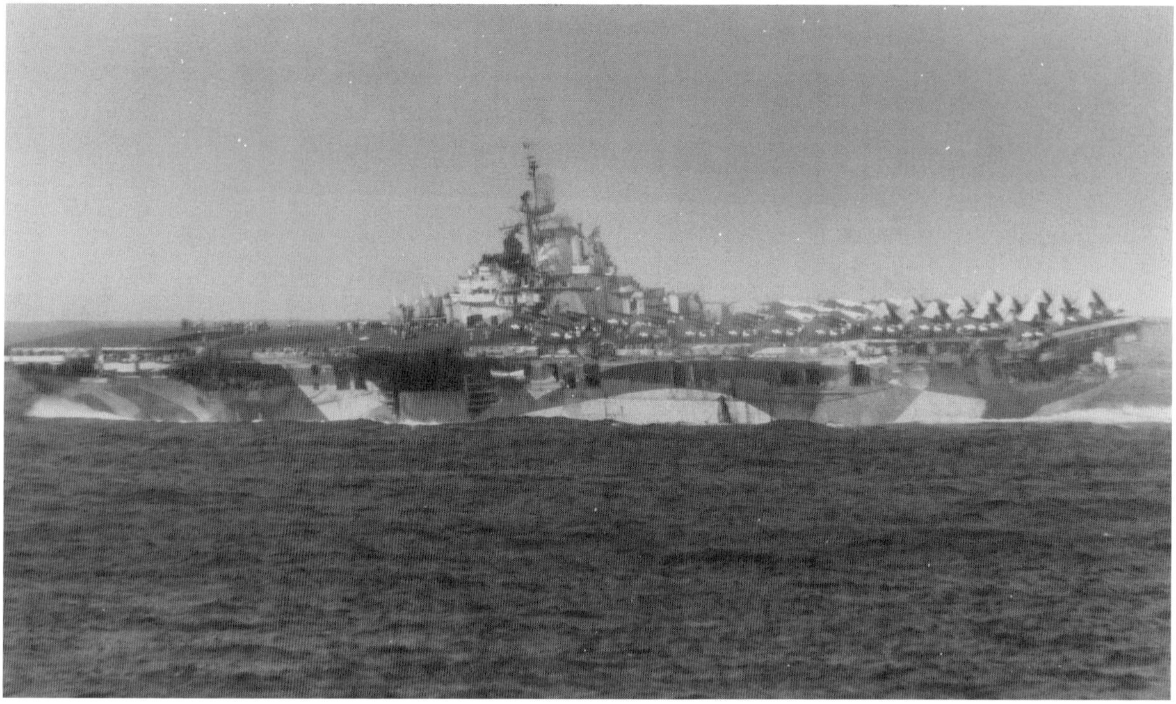

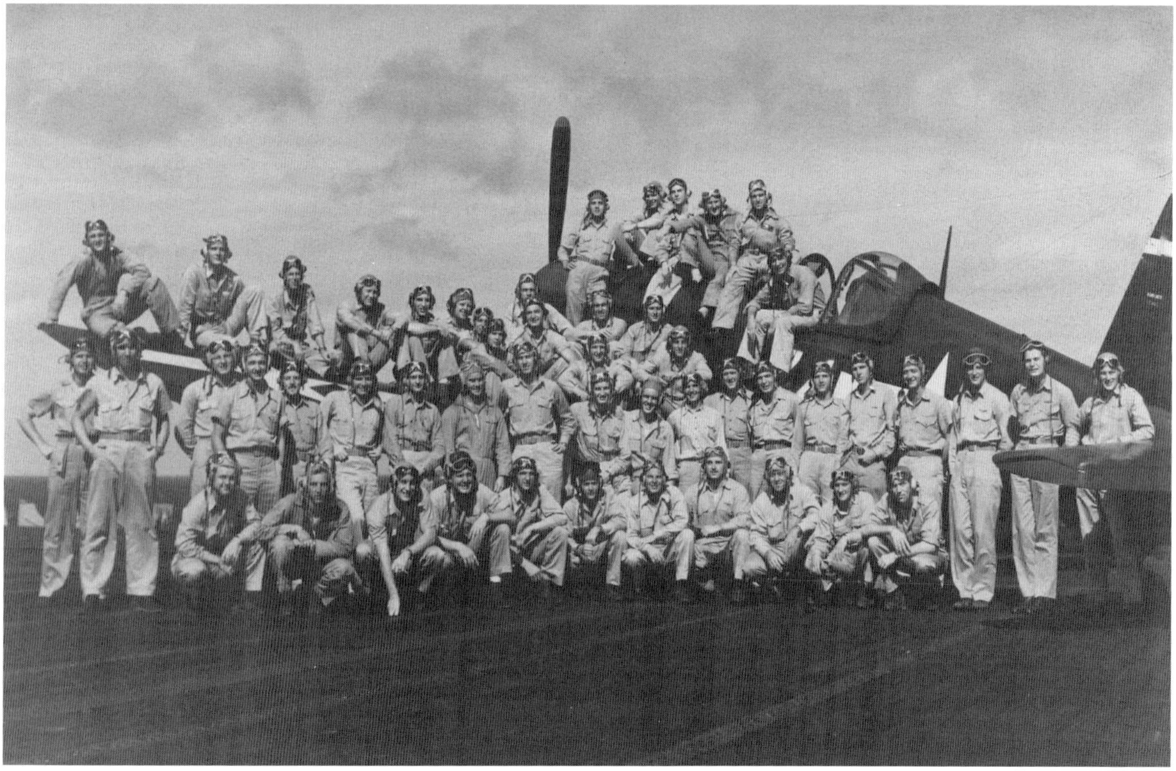

Opposite above: As a result of the kamikaze strikes *Ticonderoga* developed a significant list but was still able to steam ahead, her machinery being undamaged. Counter flooding eventually righted the ship and with the fires extinguished she withdrew to Ulithi for temporary repairs before sailing back to the US for a full refit. Fully repaired, she rejoined the fleet at Ulithi on 22 May 1945 and subsequently was part of Task Force 38 (Task Force 58 from the end of May) as they mounted operations against the Japanese homeland until the end of hostilities on 16 August 1945. (NARA)

Opposite below: In the earlier view of *Ticonderoga* viewed from the *Essex* a number of F4U Corsairs are ranged on the latter's forward flight deck. These belonged to USMC squadrons VMF-124 and 213 and are of interest as hitherto the US Navy had been reluctant to deploy Corsairs aboard carriers. However, several Marine Corps fighter squadrons were hastily embarked at the end of 1944 to boost fighter defences against the kamikaze threat and the Corsair subsequently proved to be extremely successful as a fleet-based fighter. Here the pilots of VMF-124 and 213 proudly pose in front one of their aircraft while aboard the *Essex*. (NARA)

The USS *Randolph* (CV-15) joined Task Force 58 at Ulithi early in February 1945. Later that month she participated in strikes against targets in the Tokyo area and was also involved in supporting the landings on Iwo Jima which occurred on 19 February. Returning to the supposed safety of the Ulithi anchorage, she was subjected to a surprise kamikaze attack on 11 March. The aircraft concerned was a Yokosuko P1Y (Frances) high-speed medium bomber, part of a formation that had set off from Kyushu on a one-way suicide mission. However, only one made a successful attack when it hit the carrier's starboard quarter, killing 27 men and wounding over 100 more. The damage to the ship was not too serious and this view shows the heavy repair ship USS *Jason* (ARH-1) alongside at Ulithi assisting in the remedial work. *Randolph* was able to rejoin the task force off Okinawa on 7 April. (NARA)

Above: Another casualty from the kamikaze attacks was USS *Hancock* (CV-19), which had joined the Pacific Fleet at Ulithi in October 1944. On 7 April 1945 she was part of Task Group 58.3 operating off Okinawa when she was hit by a kamikaze which sliced across the crowded flight deck, its bomb exploding on the port catapult. Despite losing sixty-one men killed and many more injured, the ship was soon back in action less than an hour after the attack. Nevertheless, she was withdrawn two days later and sailed to Pearl Harbor for repairs. By the middle of June these were completed, and she is shown here as she sailed to rejoin the fleet. Noticeable in this view is the slightly lengthened bow which allowed a better field of fire for two quadruple 40mm mountings. This modification was incorporated in all Essex class carriers completed from 1943 onwards (except CV-31 *Bon Homme Richard*) and these were referred to as the Long Hulled Essex class. (NARA)

Opposite above: The landings on Okinawa in April 1945 provoked a predictably strong reaction from the defending Japanese forces. Over the next two months until the island was secured the US Navy lost no less than thirty-four ships to both conventional and kamikaze attacks. On 11 May the *Bunker Hill* (CV-17) was hit by two kamikazes within the space of 30 seconds and both aircraft succeeded in releasing their bombs before crashing into the carrier. The result was carnage and although other ships were quickly alongside to assist in fighting fires, 390 crew were killed and another 43 were missing, presumed dead. This was a major disaster, second only to the similar fate suffered by the USS *Franklin* a few months earlier. (NARA)

Opposite below: The horrific scene aboard *Bunker Hill* in the aftermath of the kamikaze strikes. Behind the battered 40mm gun mounting sailors attend to some of the wounded while on deck the wreckage of various aircraft is visible through the smoke. Water from the fire-fighting efforts cascades off the side of the flight deck. Despite the damage, *Bunker Hill* was able to get underway at 20 knots and subsequently passed through Ulithi and Pearl Harbor on her way to Bremerton Navy Yard on the US west coast for permanent repairs. She was still in dockyard hands when the war ended on 15 August. (NARA)

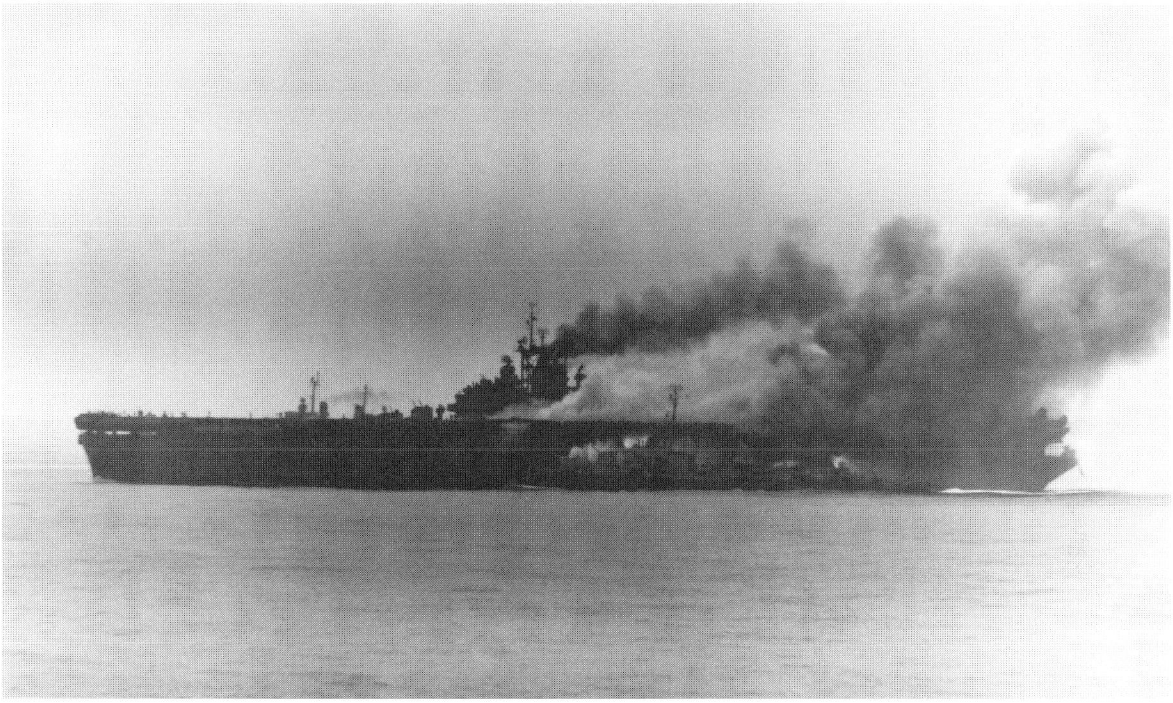

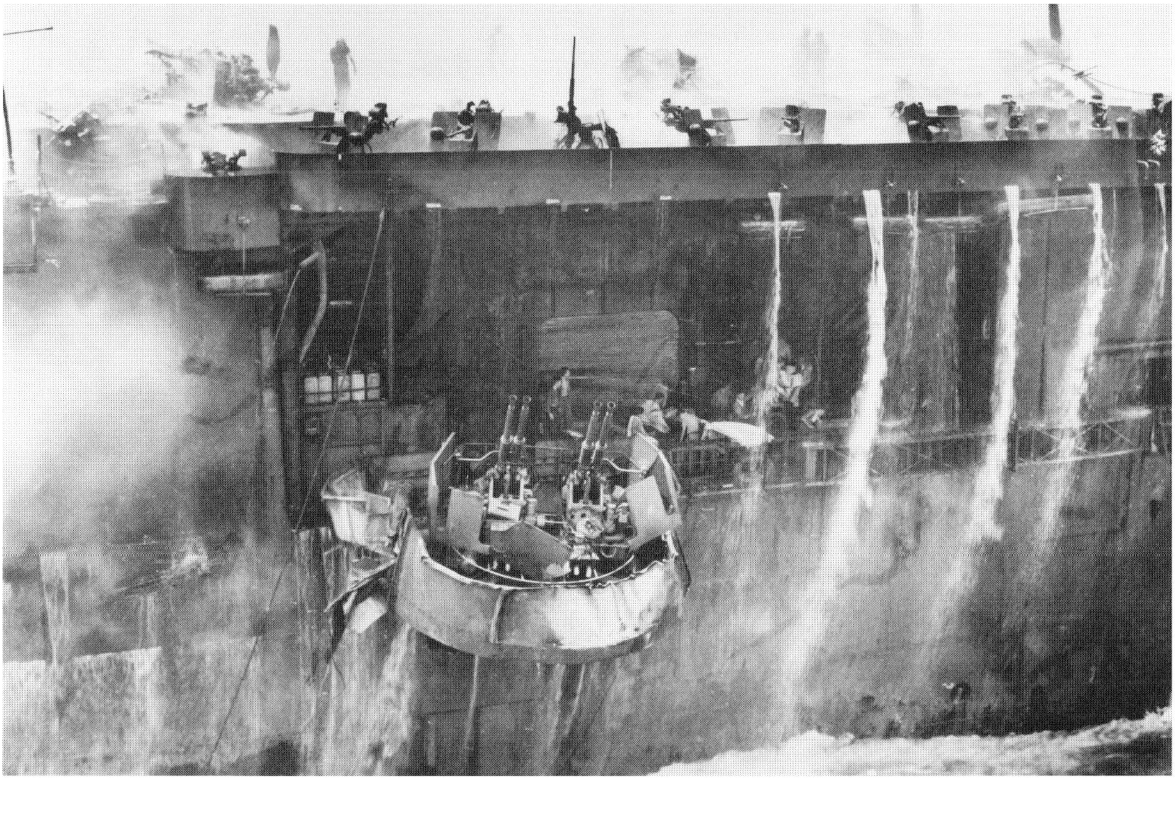

Above: Despite the damage caused by kamikazes and other attacks, the fast carriers continued to give a good account of themselves. This scoreboard aboard USS *Hornet* (CV-12) gives a detailed list of the actions in which the ship had been involved up to the beginning of May 1945. It also shows the numbers of enemy aircraft claimed as shot down by the ship's guns and the aircraft of its air group, as well as ships sunk (indicating 1 aircraft carrier, 1 light cruiser, 6 destroyers and 37 transports or merchant ships). Not bad for just one ship! (NARA)

Opposite above: It wasn't only enemy action with which the US naval forces had to contend. On 4 June 1945 the carriers USS *Hornet* (CV-12) and USS *Bennington* (CV-20) formed part of TG 38.1 operating off Japan when they ran into a typhoon. In heavy seas and winds of over 100mph several ships suffered severe damage including *Hornet*, on which the forward flight deck was wrecked. *Bennington* suffered similar damage and the heavy cruiser USS *Pittsburgh* (CA-72) lost a section of her bow. (NARA)

Opposite below: The typhoon played havoc with aircraft parked on the open flight deck. This scene of chaos shows wrecked Hellcats of VF-17 aboard the USS *Hornet*. In all about seventy-five aircraft were destroyed aboard the two Essex class carriers and the light carrier *Belleau Wood* (CVL-24) which was also attached to the task group. As the weather cleared, *Hornet* attempted to launch aircraft but the first, a Corsair, was caught by air eddies caused by the distorted flight deck and crashed into the sea. Flight operations were immediately suspended until it was arranged for *Hornet* and *Bennington* to steam astern at 18 knots and launch aircraft over the stern – a procedure for which provision was made when the ships were built but which was rarely used. (NARA)

85

Above: USS *Bennington* (CV-20) joined Task Force 58 at Ulithi in February 1945 and, along with the USS *Randolph* (CV-15), provided a welcome boost to the fast carrier force which at that stage included no less than nine Essex class carriers. Although only fully operational for the last six months of the war, the *Bennington* had an eventful time in action. She took part in operations covering the assaults on Iwo Jima and Okinawa and her aircraft participated in the sinking of the mighty battleship *Yamato* on 7 April 1945. As mentioned, she was damaged in the June typhoon but was only out of action for just over two weeks before joining in the final strikes against Japan in July and August. (NARA)

Opposite above: Yet another Essex class carrier arrived at Ulithi on 20 April 1945 in the form of the USS *Shangri-La* (CV-38), which had previously commissioned in September 1944. Her name did not follow the usual tradition of commemorating battles or previous ships but had its roots in the famous Dolittle raid in 1942 when Army B-25 bombers took off from the original USS *Hornet* (CV-8) to bomb Tokyo. When asked by a reporter where the bombers had come from, President Roosevelt replied, 'Shangri-La', a reference to a fictional land in the novel *Lost Horizons*. In that respect the adoption of the name when the ship was laid down in early 1943 was a commemoration of the raid and its gallant crews. The ship itself was soon in action off Okinawa and then took part in the final strikes against Japan. (NARA)

Opposite below: The last Essex class to join the fleet in time to see action was the USS *Bon Homme Richard* (named after the sail frigate commanded by John Paul Jones during the American War of Independence, 1775–83). After a period of training and working up, she joined Task Force 38 on 6 June 1945 and commenced a series of strikes against the Japanese home islands on 2 July which continued until the end of hostilities. Laid down in February 1943, the *Bon Homme Richard* was the last of the class to be completed with the original short bow carrying only a single 40mm quad mounting, the field of fire of which was restricted by the flight-deck overhang. (NARA)

87

Task Force 38 puts on a demonstration of power off the coast of Japan on 17 August 1945 – two days after the Japanese surrender. In the foreground is the USS *Wasp* (CV-18) while USS *Shangri-La* (CV-38) is to the left of centre. At left edge of the picture is the USS *Independence* (CVL-22) while several other unidentified carriers including other Essex class are in the background. With the war finally over, the sight of such a large armada would not be seen again as the nature of naval warfare in the atomic age had changed forever. (NHHC)

Chapter Six

The Post-war Era and Korea

With the end of the war signalled by the dropping of two atomic bombs in August 1945 two Essex class still under construction were cancelled and subsequently broken up. However, another six were subsequently completed after September 1945 giving the US Navy a total of twenty-four of this type of carrier. This was obviously far too many for a peacetime navy and after a period when some were used to repatriate US military personnel from the various wartime theatres, most were laid up in reserve. Of those in commission, some were deployed with the Atlantic and Mediterranean fleets in contrast to wartime when the Essex class had operated exclusively in the Pacific.

The introduction of jet aircraft in the late 1940s posed particular problems for their operation from the carriers and this resulted in the first of many modification schemes to adapt the ships for faster and heavier aircraft. The first of these was known as SCB-27A (SCB – Ship's Characteristics Board) and included the fitting of new more-powerful H-8 hydraulic catapults with blast deflectors behind, strengthening of sections of the flight deck, removal of the twin 5in gun turrets from the flight deck, new island superstructure incorporating an integrated smoke stack, increased stowage for aviation fuel and numerous detailed changes to facilitate handling the aircraft. To maintain stability the hull was bulged, increasing beam to 101ft at the waterline. These changes were incorporated in nine ships (including *Oriskany*, which was only completed in 1950) between 1948 and 1953.

The sudden outbreak of the Korean War in June 1951 took the US and its allies by surprise and the only carriers immediately available were the USS *Valley Forge* (CV-45) and the British light fleet carrier HMS *Triumph*. These combined to form Task Force 77 and subsequently eleven Essex class operated under that command between 1951 and July 1953 when the ceasefire and armistice was arranged. Normally two were on station off the north-east coast of Korea but on occasions three or even four would be available for specific operations. The task mostly comprised close air support of UN troops fighting ashore as the war ebbed and flowed the length of the Korean peninsula and for this task the piston-engined Douglas AD Skyraider proved to be ideal as it could carry a much heavier ordnance load than other

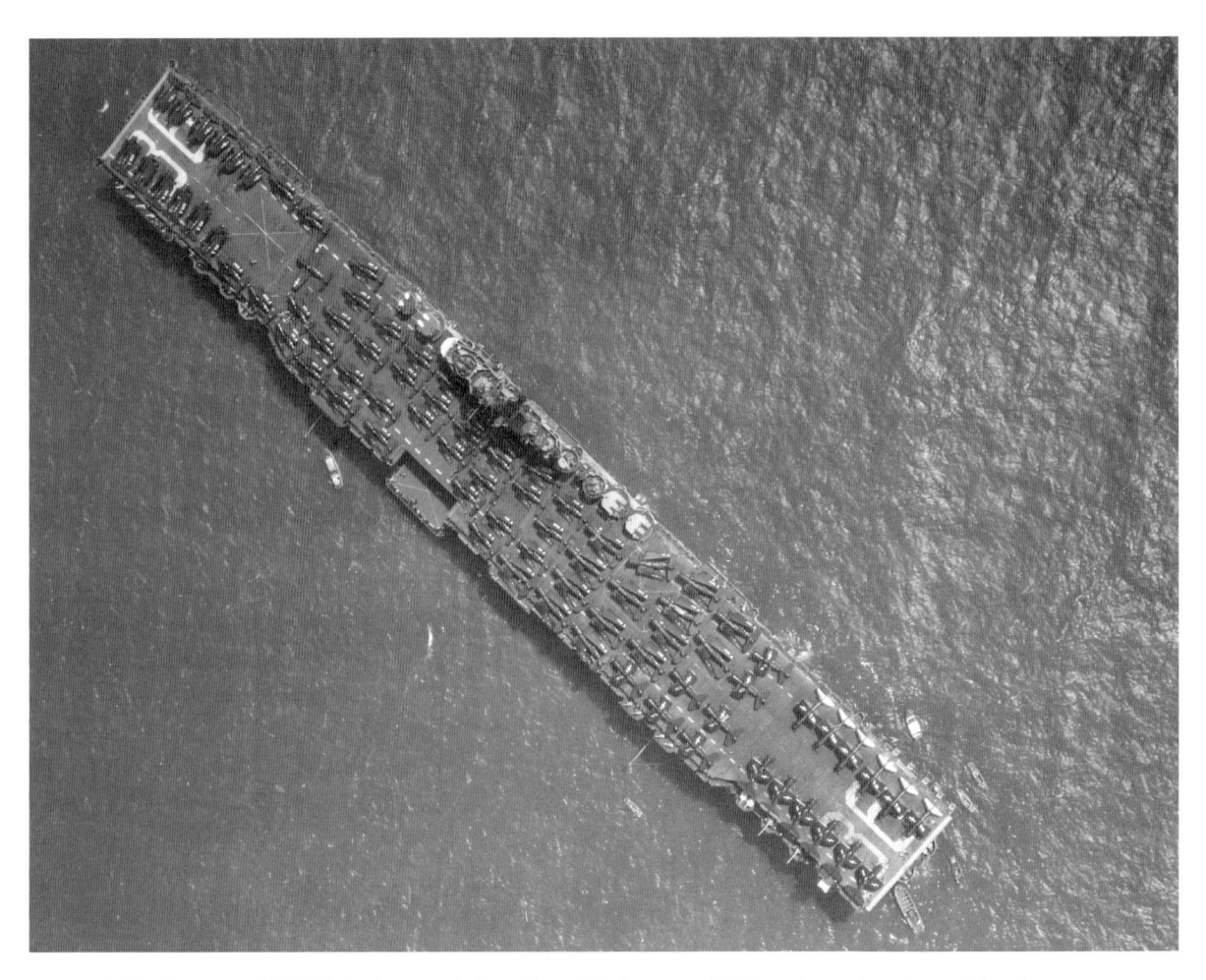

USS *Antietam* (CV-36) had commissioned on 28 January 1945 and on the day of the Japanese surrender she was en route from Pearl Harbor to join the US Third Fleet. Although too late to see any combat, she remained in Chinese and Japanese waters for the next three years supporting Allied forces that had occupied territories liberated from Japanese occupation, including Korea, Manchuria and Northern China. It was not until June 1949 that she returned to the US and was decommissioned, although she was later to play a pioneering role in the development of jet operations from aircraft carriers. This photo was taken at Norfolk VA in May 1945 before her deployment to the Pacific. Ranged on deck are Curtiss Helldivers and Grumman Avengers for delivery to Hawaii as reinforcements for the Pacific Fleet air groups. (NARA)

available aircraft. The Panther jet fighter was mostly employed in the escort and flak suppression roles but was outclassed by the MiG-15s flown by North Korean and Chinese pilots. Nevertheless, the generally higher standard of training of the US Navy pilots meant that they were not completely overwhelmed and indeed occasionally managed to shoot down a MiG. Towards the end of the war the UN command authorised the destruction of the North Korean power supplies, and most of the generating stations as well as some dams were completely destroyed. In this campaign the Skyraiders, along with other USAF bombers, played a significant role. The fact that the US Navy was unlikely to be opposed by any significant enemy naval force, together with the emphasis on attacking land targets as demonstrated by the Korean War, led in 1952 to the Essex class being redesignated as Attack Carriers (CVA).

Another carrier which had been intended to join the task forces covering Operation Olympic was USS *Lake Champlain* (CV-39), which commissioned on 3 June 1945 and is shown here at Norfolk VA in August 1945 with her air group embarked prior to deployment to the Pacific. However, with the ending of hostilities her aircraft were disembarked, and she was fitted out as a troop transport. In this guise she was allocated to Operation Magic Carpet (the repatriation of US troops from Europe) and continued in this role until placed in reserve in February 1947. (NHHC)

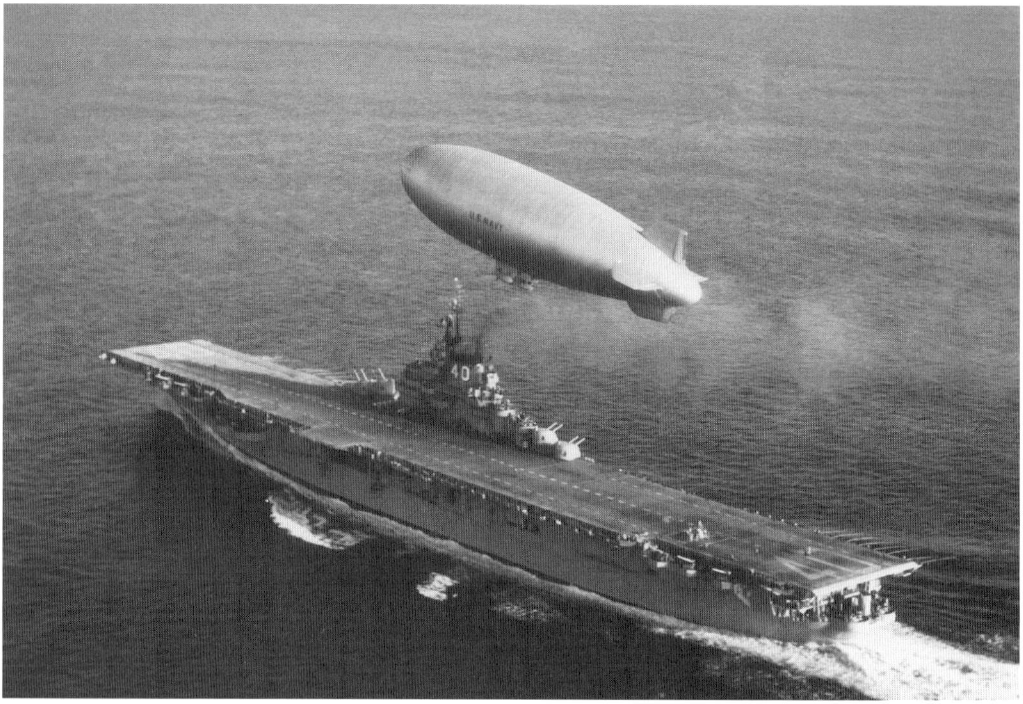
40

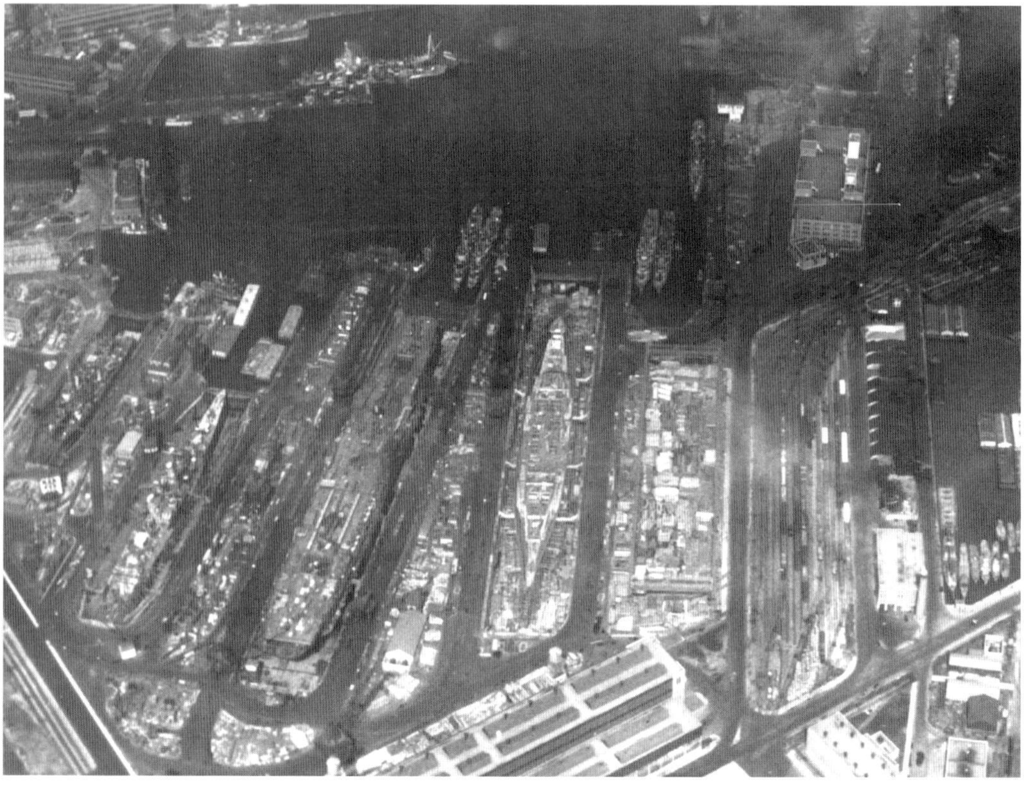

Above: The Grumman F6F Hellcat formed the backbone of the fighter force aboard US carriers between 1943 and 1945. Although a tough and capable fighter with a good turn of speed, it was not endowed with a startling rate of climb. However, as early as 1943 Grumman began work on a lightweight development, the prime function of which would be to act as a fast-climbing interceptor. This resulted in the F8F Bearcat, which was just entering service as the war ended. It was 40mph faster than the Hellcat and its initial rate of climb at 4,570ft/min was a 50 per cent improvement. Shown here is an F8F-2 Bearcat preparing to take off from USS *Valley Forge* (CV-45) in September 1949, by which time no less than twenty-four US Navy squadrons were equipped with this nimble fighter. (NARA)

Opposite above: Despite the end of the war work continued on completing several Essex class then under construction. The two most advanced were *Princeton* (CV-37) and *Tarawa* (CV-40), which commissioned on 18 November and 8 December 1945 respectively. The latter served mostly in the Atlantic and Caribbean and consequently was the only Essex class carrier never to be engaged in actual combat operations. Also, unlike her sister ships, she underwent no major modernisation refits and retained her original Second World War appearance throughout her career as illustrated by this 1954 view of the ship. Overhead is a ZSG-4 US Navy non-rigid airship of which fifteen were delivered from 1953 onwards, some remaining in service as late as 1962. (NARA)

Opposite below: The USS *Reprisal* (CV-35) and USS *Iwo Jima* (CV-46) had been laid down in July 1944 and January 1945 but with the end of the war both were cancelled on 11–12 August 1945. The incomplete hulls were eventually scrapped in 1949. This aerial view of the New York Naval Yard at Brooklyn was taken on 15 April 1945 and in the right-hand dock is the partially completed hull of the USS *Reprisal* which has yet to reach flight-deck level. To the left of her is the more advanced USS *Franklin D. Roosevelt* (CVB-42), which is being prepared for launching. She was one of three Midway class carriers which, as can be seen, were considerably larger than the Essex class. (NHHC)

94

Above: This aerial view of USS *Kearsarge* with her air group, consisting of Bearcats, Avengers and Helldivers, ranged on deck shows the ship at anchor while on a visit to Greece in September 1948. Note the forward and deck-edge lifts both left in the lowered position while a solitary Avenger stands on the after lift. (NARA)

Opposite above: Commissioned in March 1946, the USS *Kearsarge* (CV-33) is shown here while deployed with the US Sixth Fleet in the Mediterranean in 1948. Overhead a flight of four Curtiss SB2C Helldivers flown by VA-34 prepare to turn into the landing circuit while several F8F Bearcats are spotted on the forward section of the flight deck. This was something of a swansong for the Helldiver which was withdrawn from front-line service at the end of that year. (NARA)

Opposite below: The replacement for the Helldiver was the Douglas Skyraider which had flown in prototype form in March 1945. At that time, it was designated as a Torpedo Bomber (BT2D)) but almost immediately it was redesignated in the newly formulated Attack category as the AD-1. In contrast to earlier aircraft in this role it was a single-seater, a move to save weight which enabled the Skyraider to carry up to 8,000lb of ordnance. It was to prove a highly successful aircraft and over 3,000 were delivered up to 1957. This example is taking off from USS *Kearsarge* in late 1948. (NARA)

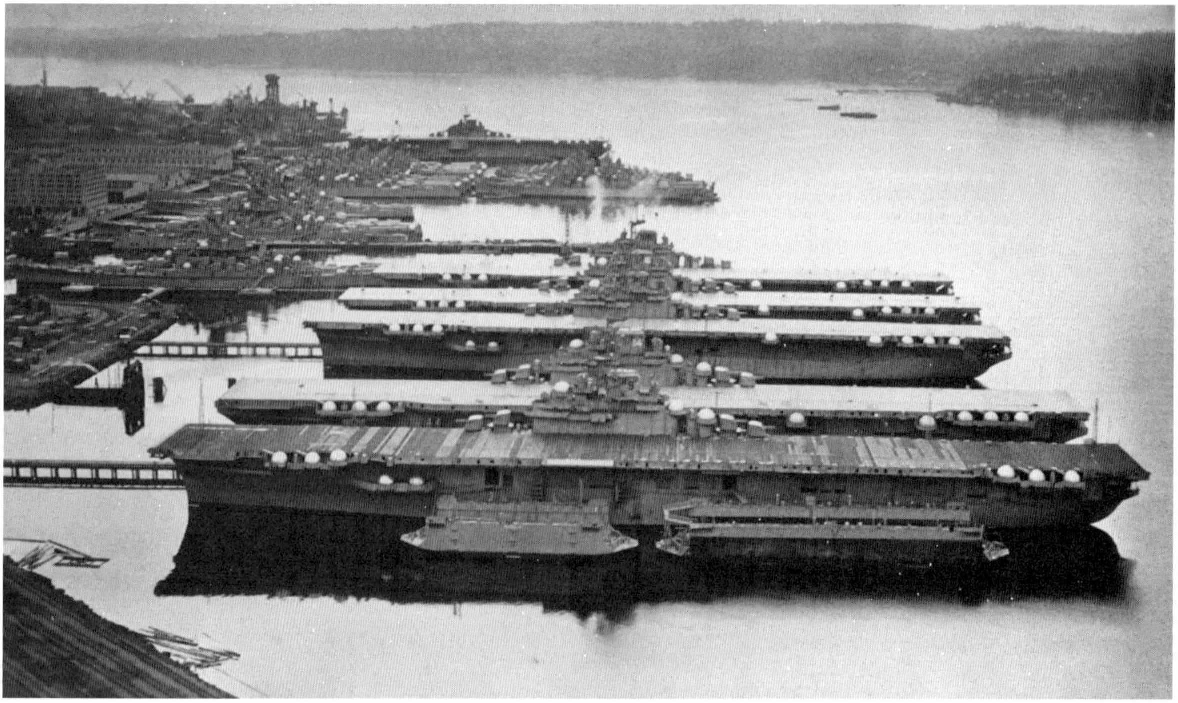

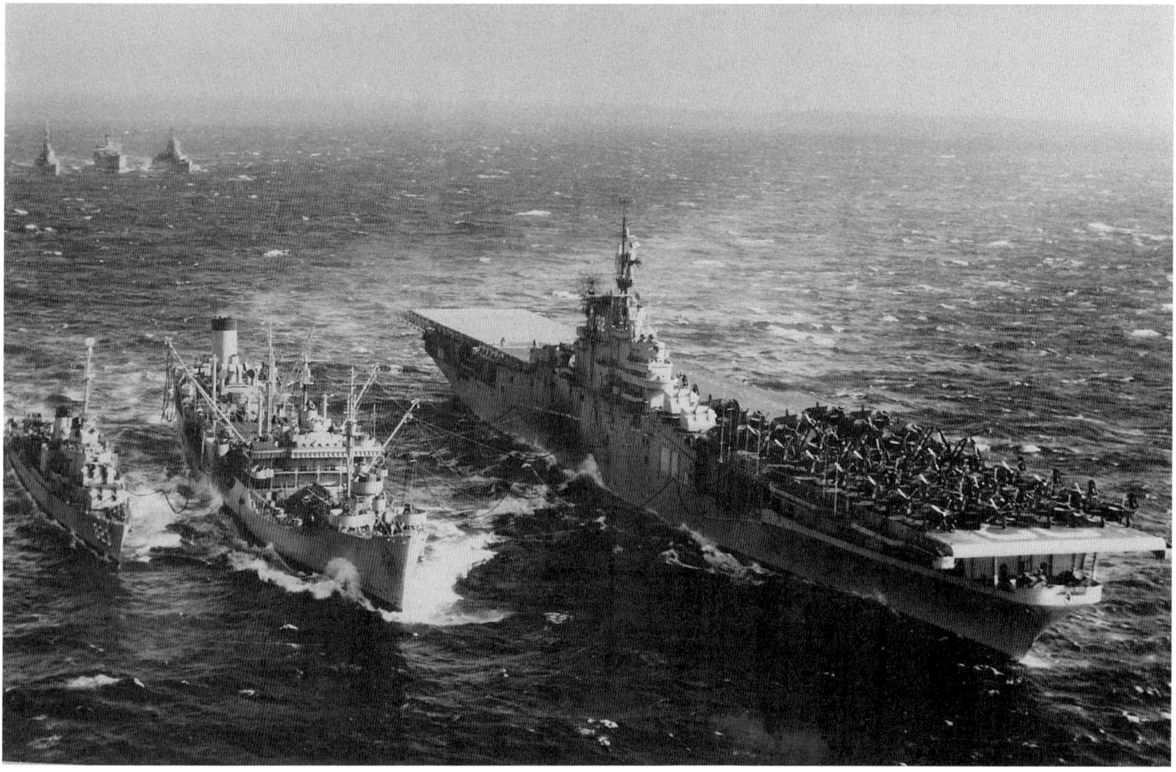

Above: The USS *Philippine Sea* (CV-47) was one of four Essex class which were completed in 1946 and she commissioned on 11 May of that year. In the late 1940s she made two deployments to the US Sixth Fleet in the Mediterranean and is here passing Gibraltar in January 1949 shortly after having carried out exercises with British carriers in the east Atlantic. Carrier Air Group 7 (CVG-7) is embarked and some of the F8F Bearcats are ranged on the forward flight deck while aft are SB2C Helldivers and TBM Avengers. (NARA)

Opposite above: In the immediate aftermath of the war many Essex class carriers were utilised as transports to bring home troops from overseas theatres while others played a role in supporting various occupation forces. However, it was inevitable that a peacetime navy would not require the great armadas deployed during hostilities and by 1947 many of the carriers which had seen arduous wartime service were laid up in reserve. This photo of Washington Naval Yard later that year shows (from front to rear) *Essex*, *Ticonderoga*, *Yorktown*, *Lexington* and *Bunker Hill*. Also, in the distant background is *Bon Homme Richard*. Although most Essex class would later be re-activated, the two carriers that had been most seriously damaged (*Franklin* and *Bunker Hill*) were never recommissioned. (NHHC)

Opposite below: In general the US Navy retained the newest Essex class in service after the war. This is USS *Leyte* (CV-32) which had commissioned in April 1946 and is shown here in early 1949 while on a training exercise in the Atlantic. The aircraft on deck are mostly F8F Bearcats as well as a few F4U Corsairs and TBM Avengers. In the centre the fleet oiler USS *Caloosahatchee* (AO-98) conducts a RAS serial with the carrier and the Gearing class destroyer USS *Samuel B. Roberts* (DD823). (NARA)

Above: Although commissioned in April 1945, the USS *Boxer* (CV-21) was not fully operational in time to see combat in the Second World War. However, she had a very active post-war career and in early 1950 was engaged in joint exercises with the British carrier HMS *Triumph* off Hong Kong. This photo of *Boxer*'s flight deck at that time shows F8F Hellcats of CVG-19 in the foreground and AD Skyraiders ranged aft. Between the two groups of US Navy aircraft are six Royal Navy Seafire 47s of 800 NAS and four Firefly FR.1s of 827 NAS. (NARA)

Opposite above: A Royal Navy Fairey Firefly FR.1 of 827 NAS taking off from USS *Boxer*, March 1950. The unusual sight of a British aircraft aboard a US Navy carrier has obviously generated a lot of interest as evidenced by the numerous 'goofers' occupying vantage points on the island superstructure. (NARA)

Opposite below: The most significant, even revolutionary, factor in the development of post-war naval aviation was the introduction of jet combat aircraft. The US Navy's first jet fighter was the McDonnell FH-1 Phantom of which the prototype shown here first flew in January 1945. Although it never entered operational service, a trials squadron was equipped with the Phantom in 1947–9 and spent short periods at sea to investigate the issues arising from operating jet aircraft aboard a carrier. Although Phantoms never flew from an Essex class carrier, the lessons learned were to have a profound effect on their future careers. (Aviation Archives)

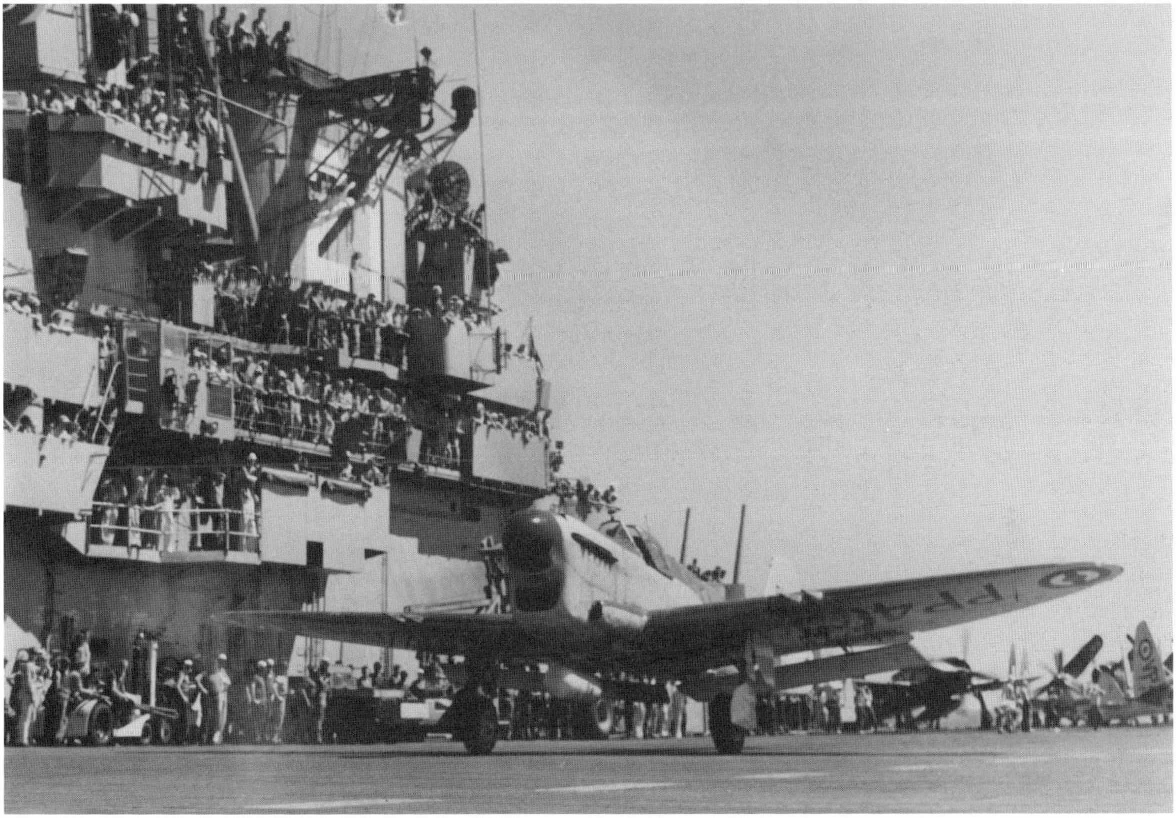

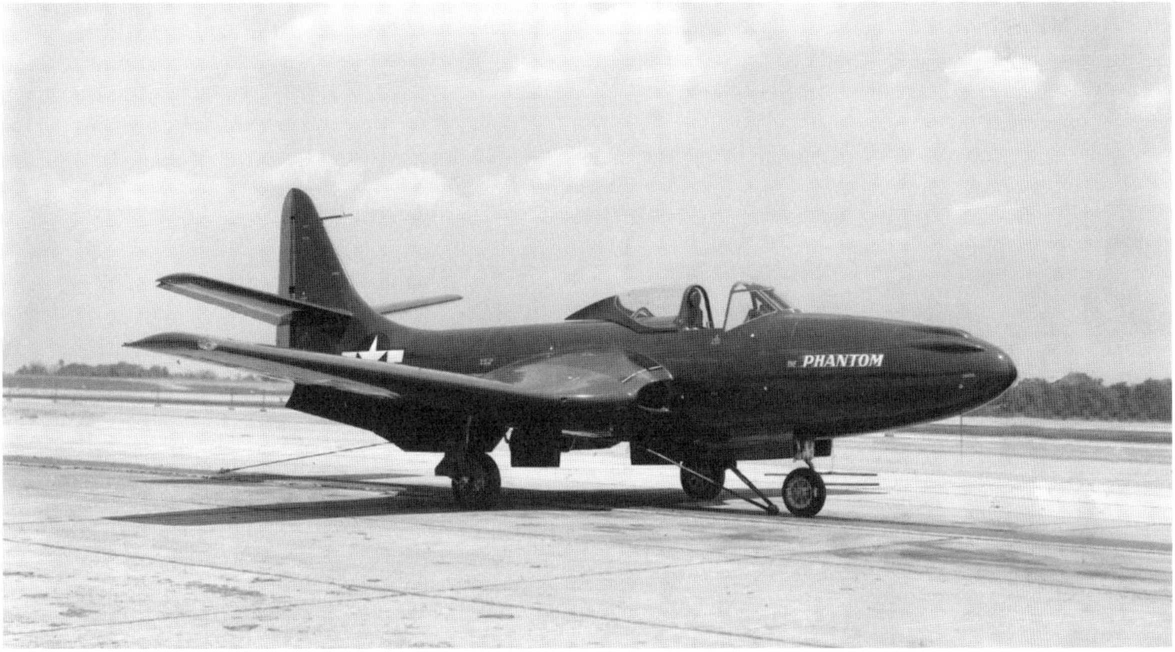
PHANTOM

The US Navy's first fully operational jet fighter was the North American FJ-1 Fury which first flew in November 1946 and flight trials revealed no serious problems. Consequently, it equipped a new squadron (VF-5A), which joined USS Boxer (CV-21) in March 1948 and remained aboard as part of the ship's air group until the end of 1949. This was the first deployment of a carrier-borne jet-fighter squadron and was a notable achievement. One of its aircraft is shown taking off in March shortly after the squadron had joined the ship. At this stage most take-offs were free run (as opposed to a catapult launch) and one drawback of the jets was that they required a much longer take-off run, reducing the space available to park other aircraft. (NARA)

The FJ-1 Fury enabled the US Navy to gain experience of operating jet fighters at sea but only thirty were produced. In March 1949 the Navy received the first of 1,382 Grumman F9F Panthers, which became the standard jet fighter in the carrier air groups and played a major role in the Korean War. By the end of that conflict most of the Essex class carriers involved embarked two, or even three, squadrons of Panthers. Here a Panther has just landed aboard USS *Boxer* (CV-21) in May 1951 and a flight-deck crewman stands at left ready to indicate when the arrester hook has been disengaged so that the pilot can taxi forward to clear the deck for the next landing aircraft. (NARA)

102

Opposite: The operation of jet aircraft from Essex class carriers required significant modifications which were applied under the SBC-27A scheme. The first of the class to undergo this conversion was *Essex* herself, which having been placed in reserve in January 1947 was reactivated two years later and docked at Puget Sound Naval Ship Yard for work to begin. This view shows her in dry dock and already the deck-mounted 5in guns have been removed and sections of the forward flight deck have also been removed to allow for the installation of more powerful catapults. (NARA)

Essex (CV-9) recommissioned on 15 January 1951 and some of the changes incorporated in the SCB-27A scheme can be seen. Most notable are the deletion of the deck-mounted 5in gun to provide more deck space and the fairing of the funnel with its raked cap into the bridge structure. New radars include an SPS-6 search radar and an SPS-8 height-finding radar. The close-range AA armament of 40mm and 20mm guns has been replaced by a total of fourteen 3in/50cal twin mountings, two of which are on the bow and some of the others are visible in sponsons on the side of the hull below the island superstructure. (NARA)

Above: Another view of *Essex* as modified under SBC-27A with a crowded flight deck, including the Grumman F9F Panther jet fighters of VF-172 behind which are F4U Corsairs and AD Skyraiders. Clearly shown are the two twin automatic 3in/50cal gun mountings on the bow. This photograph was taken in June 1951 just as the North Korean invasion of South Korea triggered the three years of war in which several Essex class carriers were to be in action. (NARA)

Opposite above: Despite the advent of jets, piston-engined aircraft such as the Vought F4U Corsair shown here taking off from the USS *Boxer* (CV-21) in July 1951 were still able to play an important role. With a speed in excess of 400mph, armed with six 0.5in machine guns or four 20mm cannon and able to carry up to 2,000lb bombs, the highly manoeuvrable Corsair was much in demand in the ground-attack role. This example belongs to VF-791, and the propeller leaves a spiral of condensation trails due to humid conditions at the time. (NARA)

Opposite below: One of *Boxer*'s Corsairs is manhandled onto the lift which will carry it up to the flight deck. It has been prepared for a strike against a Korean target and carries eight 250lb bombs on underwing racks as well as two long-range drop tanks under the wing centre section. (NARA)

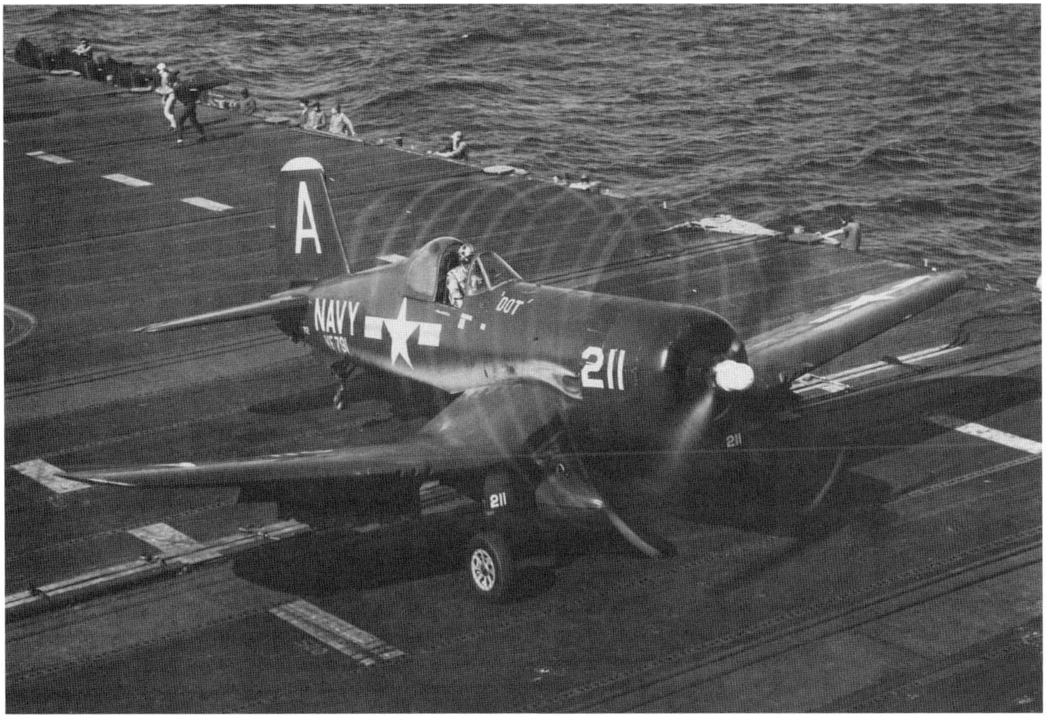
A
NAVY
'DOT'
211
211
211

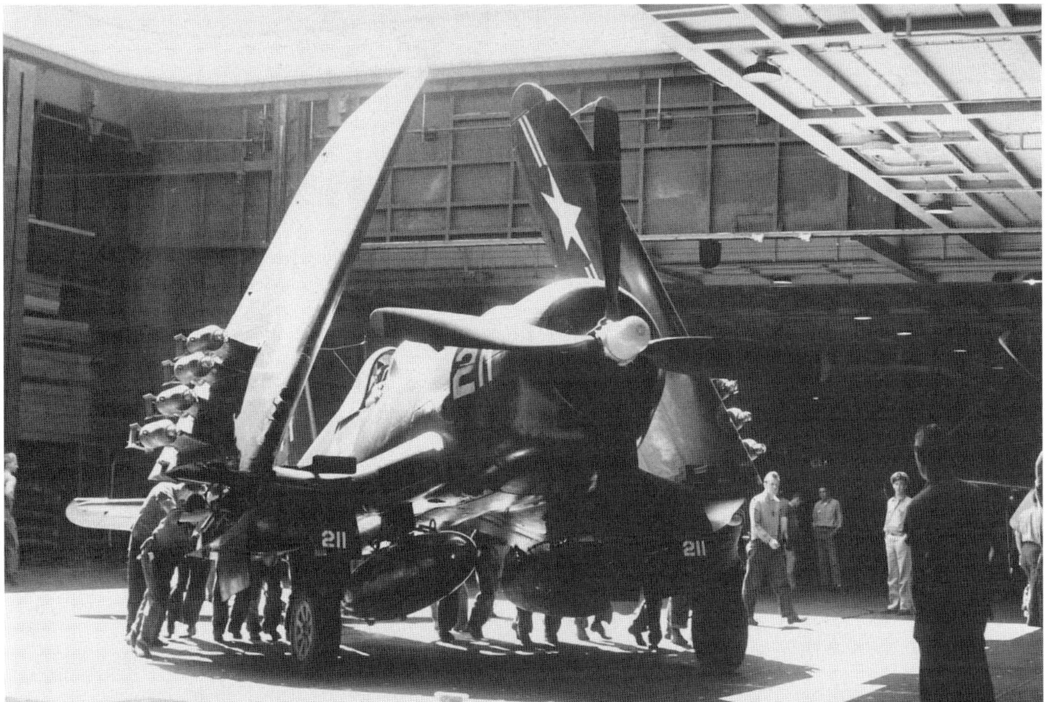
211
211
211

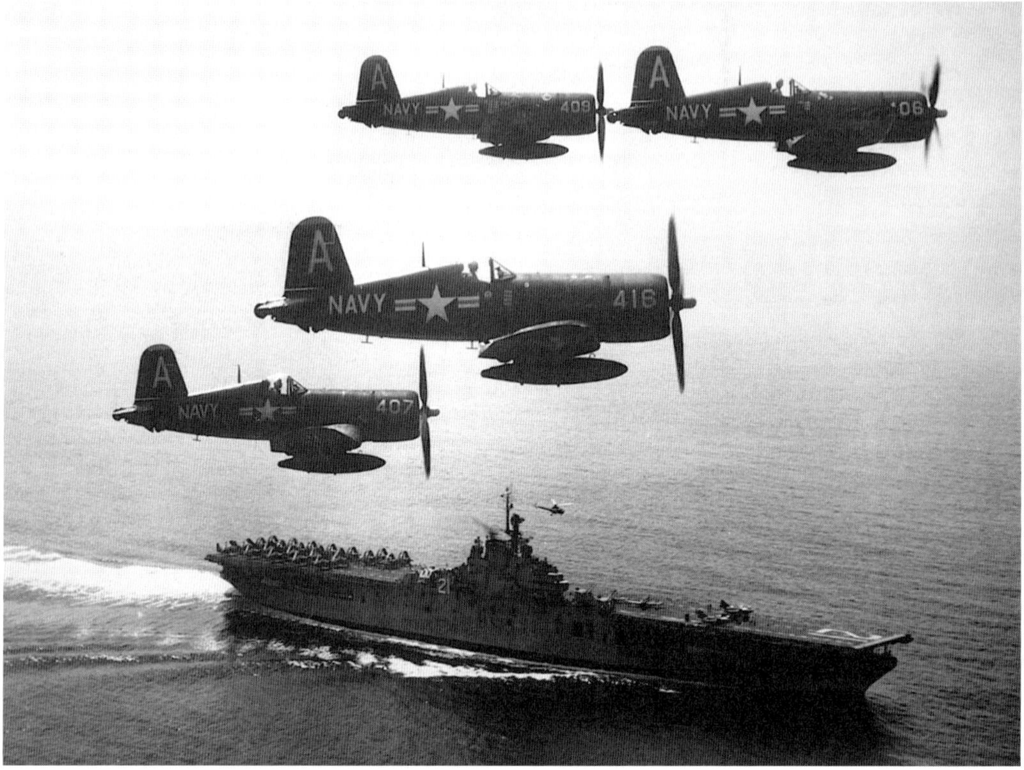
A
NAVY
416
407
21

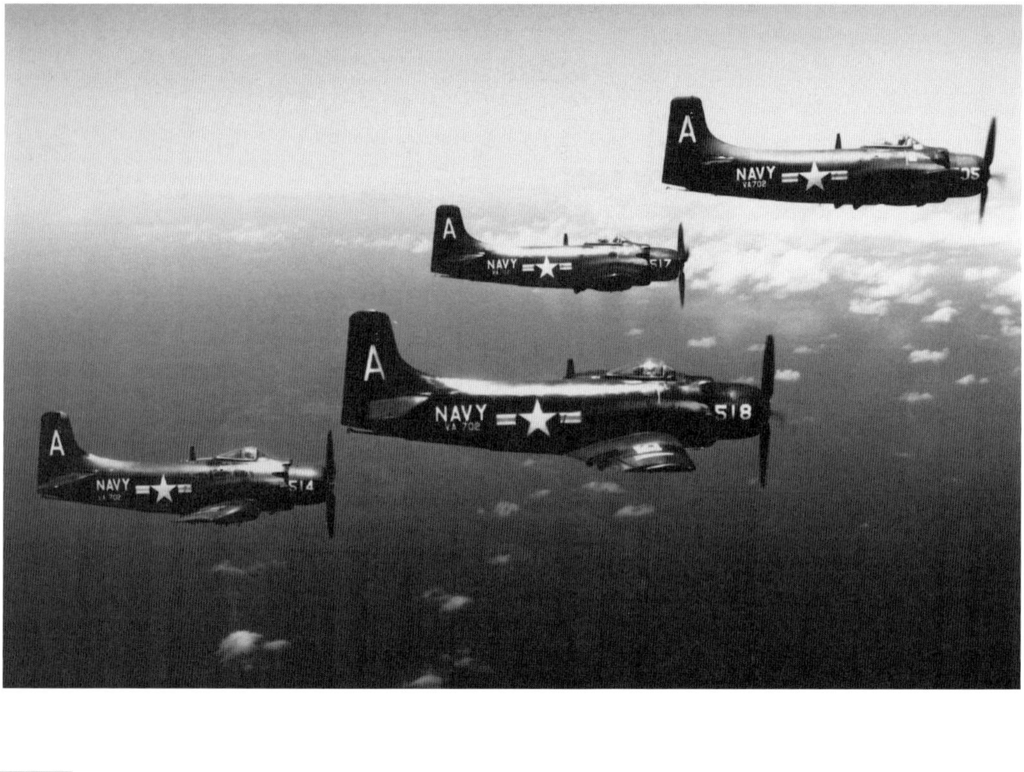
A
NAVY
VA 702
518
514

The USS *Boxer* (CV-21) was one of the most active US Navy carriers during the Korean War, making four separate deployments between 1950 and 1953. This overhead view was taken in September 1952 when the ship was nearing the end of her third Korean deployment. Ranged aft on the flight deck are some of the aircraft from her air group (CVG-2), including Skyraiders of VA-65 and Corsairs from the four fighter squadrons embarked (VF-21, 22, 63, and 64). (NARA)

Opposite above: A formation of Corsairs flown by VF884 returning from a strike over Korea circle USS *Boxer* awaiting the launch of a flight of Panther jets to be completed before the deck can be cleared for landings. Note also the Sikorsky HO3S helicopter hovering off the port side of the flight deck. The use of helicopters for plane guard duties instead of the traditional destroyer was introduced at this time and meant that the crews of ditched aircraft could be rescued much more quickly. (NHHC)

Opposite below: The other piston-engined stalwart was the Douglas AD Skyraider which excelled in the ground-attack role. This formation of Skyraiders from VA-702 aboard USS *Boxer* is heading towards targets in Korea in September 1951. VA-702 was actually a naval reserve squadron and, at the time, *Boxer*'s air group was composed entirely of reserve squadrons – this first time this had occurred. (NARA)

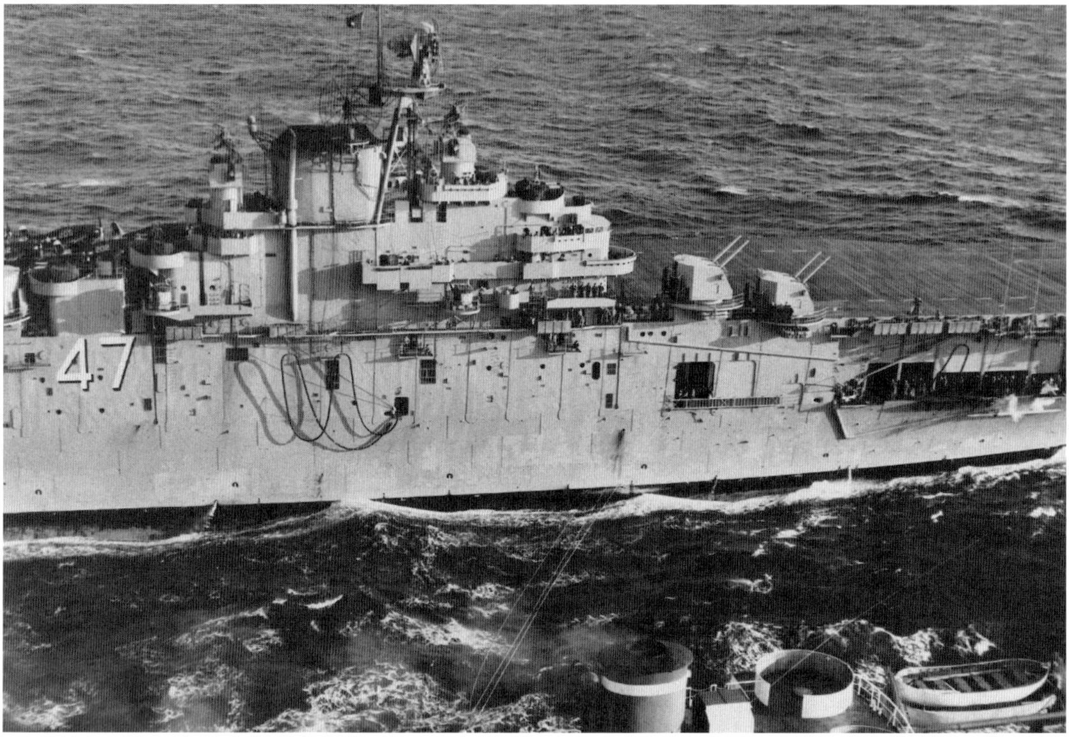
47

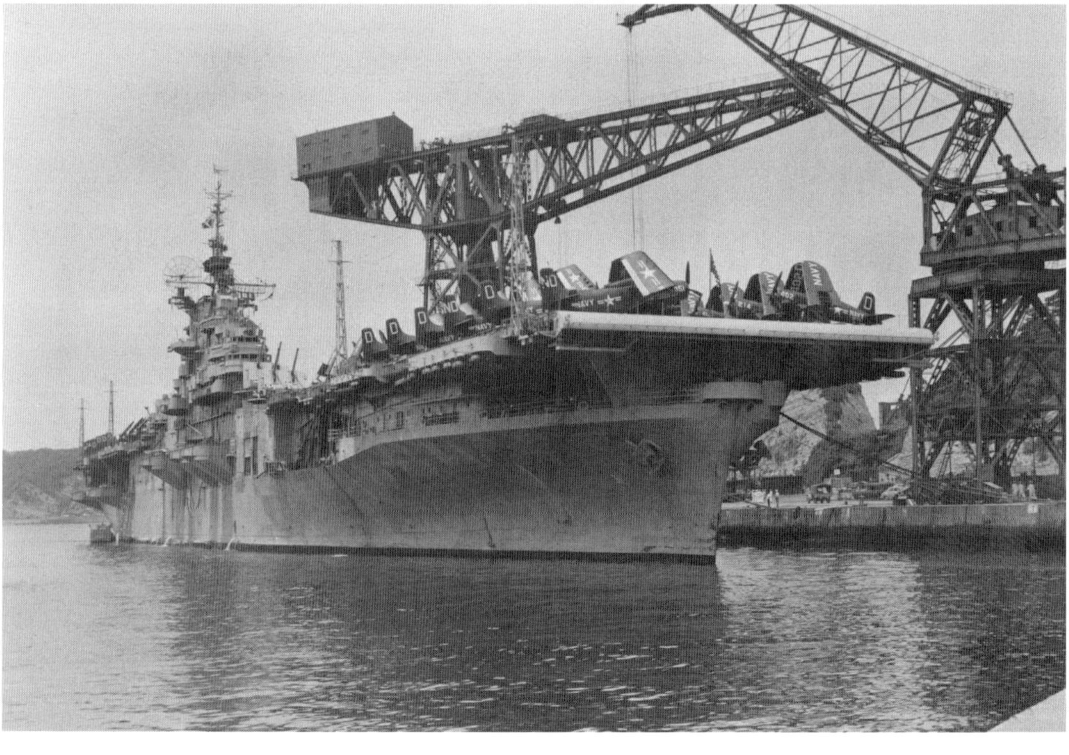
NAVY

Above: The USS *Valley Forge* (CV-45) was completed too late for war service and was not commissioned until 3 November 1946. Almost a year later, on 9 October 1947, she left her home port of San Diego for Hawaii where she spent three months on training exercises. Subsequently, she proceeded to the Far East where she exercised with the Royal Australian Navy and RN units before continuing westbound via Singapore, Ceylon (Sri Lanka) and Saudi Arabia. Passing through the Suez Canal, she exercised with the US Sixth Fleet in the Mediterranean and then visited Norway and the UK before crossing the Atlantic to New York. She completed her round-the-world cruise at San Diego on 11 June 1948 after passing through the Panama Canal and received an enthusiastic welcome, as shown here. (NARA)

Opposite above: A close-up view taken from an accompanying fleet oiler in the spring of 1949 showing the island superstructure of the USS *Philippine Sea* (CV-47), which commissioned on 11 May 1946. In common with the other Essex class completed after the war, the light AA armament was considerably reduced. For example, the quadruple 40mm mountings carried in sponsons on the side of the hull have been omitted (compare with the similar view of USS *Yorktown* on p. 54). Unlike most of her sister ships, *Philippine Sea* remained substantially unmodified throughout her career until she was laid up in reserve in 1959 (scrapped in 1971). (NARA)

Opposite below: In common with several other Essex class, the outbreak of the Korean War resulted in the USS *Bon Homme Richard* (CV-31) being taken out of reserve and she recommissioned on 15 January 1951. Subsequently she served two long deployments off Korea and this view shows her alongside at Yokosuka in 1951 during a well-deserved break from operations. During the period May to December 1951 the *Bon Homme Richard* lost twenty aircraft and five aircrew, the highest of any of the seven Essex class in action during that time. This was possibly a reflection of the fact that the ship was on station for most of that period and was heavily involved in the strike programme. On deck are Skyraiders and Corsairs of CVG-102. (NARA)

Above: In August 1950 the USS *Lake Champlain* was taken out of reserve to undergo modification to SCB-27A standards and eventually recommissioned on 19 September 1952. She reached Korean waters just in time to participate in combat action during June and July 1953, when hostilities were halted. She remained attached to the US Seventh Fleet until relieved by the USS *Kearsarge* (CV-33) on 11 October and returned home via Singapore, Suez and through the Mediterranean. In this view she is underway in the South China Sea en route to Singapore and on deck are the Panthers, Banshees and Corsairs of CVG-4. The photograph also clearly shows the revised profile of the island superstructure and faired funnel, characteristic of the SBC-27A conversions. (NARA)

Opposite above: The Sikorsky S-51 helicopter first flew in 1946 and was ordered by the US Navy as the HO3S-1, entering service with VX-3 in May 1947. It was widely used in the rescue role aboard the aircraft carriers operating off Korea and many pilots of ditched aircraft owed their lives to the skill and bravery of these pioneer helicopter pilots who often carried out dramatic rescues under fire. This example belonging to VX-3 is shown departing from USS *Kearsarge* (CV-33) during trials carried out in 1948. (NARA)

Opposite below: USS *Bon Homme Richard* (CV-31) returned for a second Korean deployment in June 1952 and this view giving a good impression of the hangar space available dates from the following November. Stowed aircraft belong to CVG-7, with a line of F9F Panthers on the left and two lines of F4U Corsairs on the right. (NHHC)

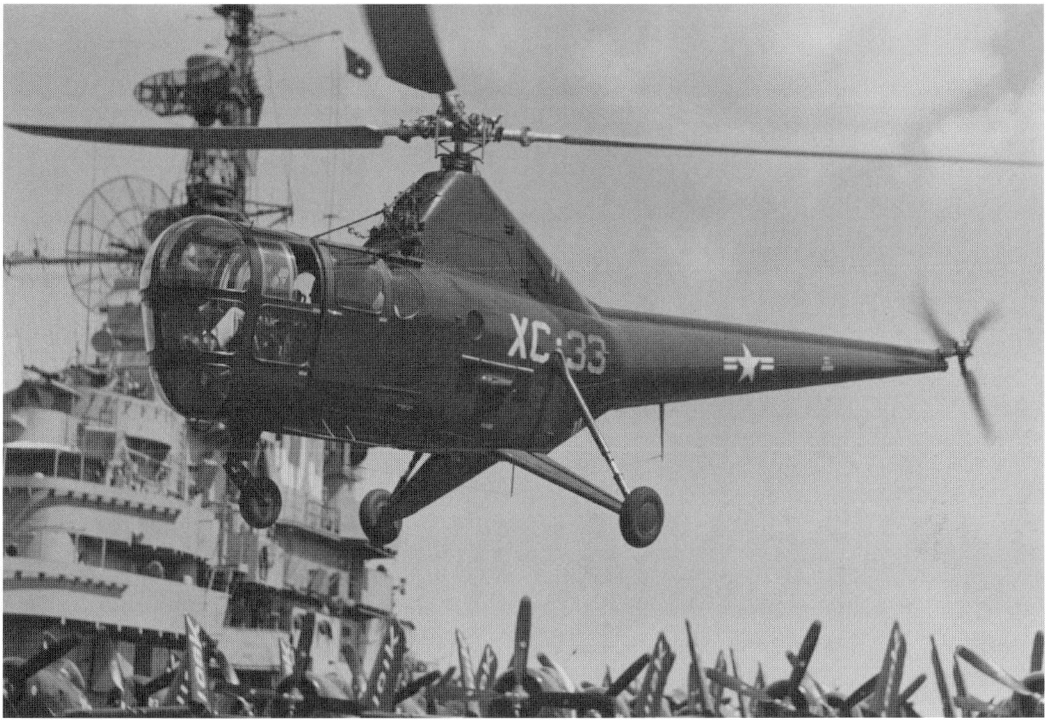
XC 33

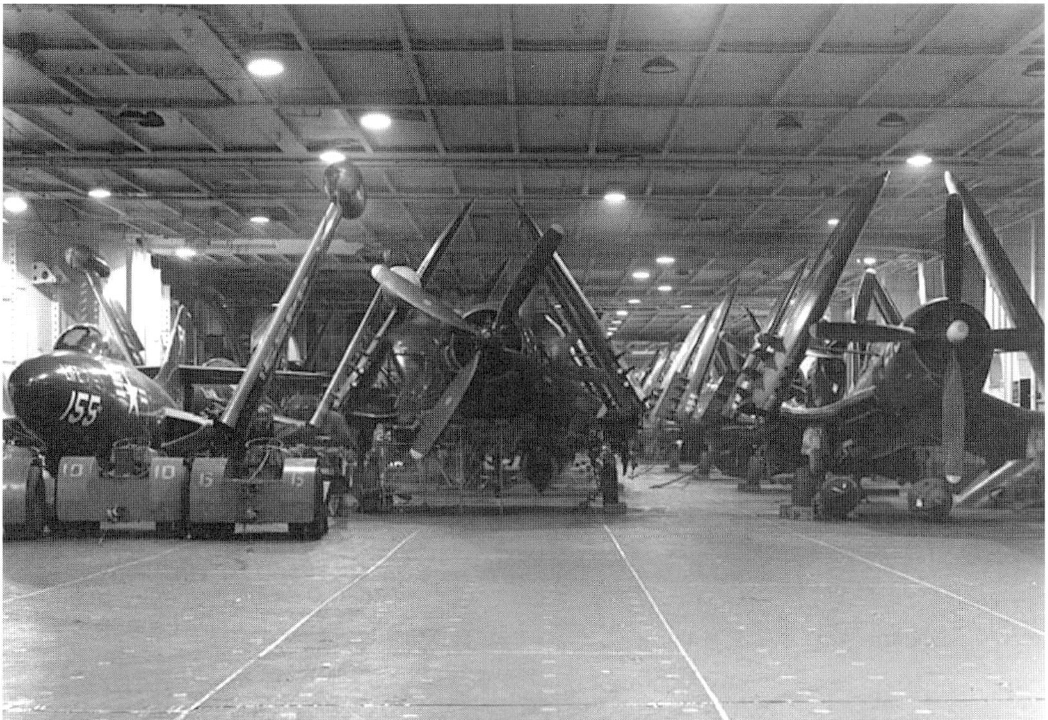
155

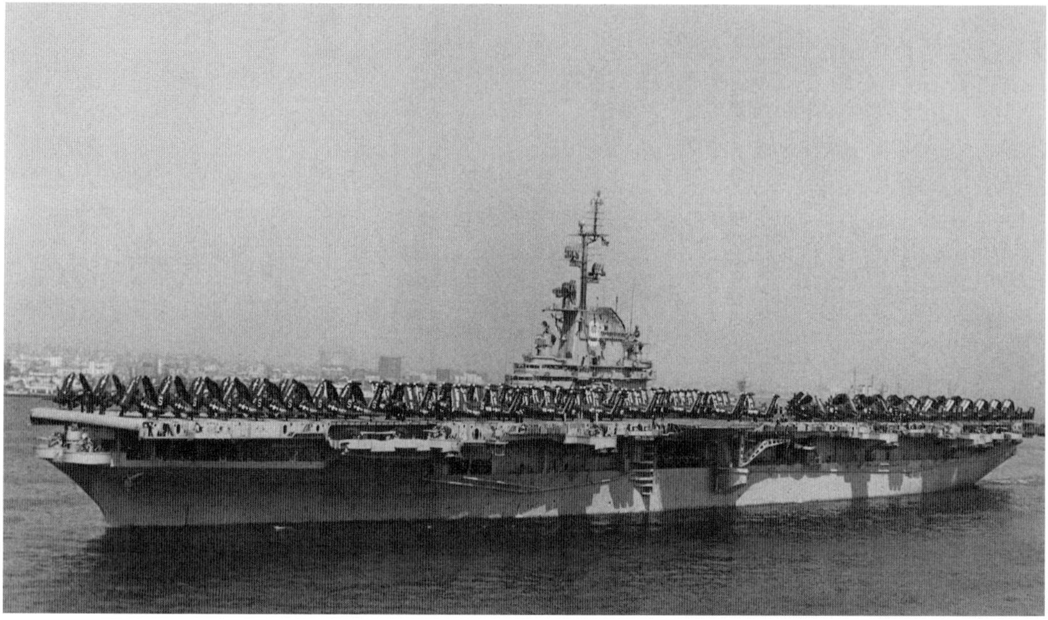

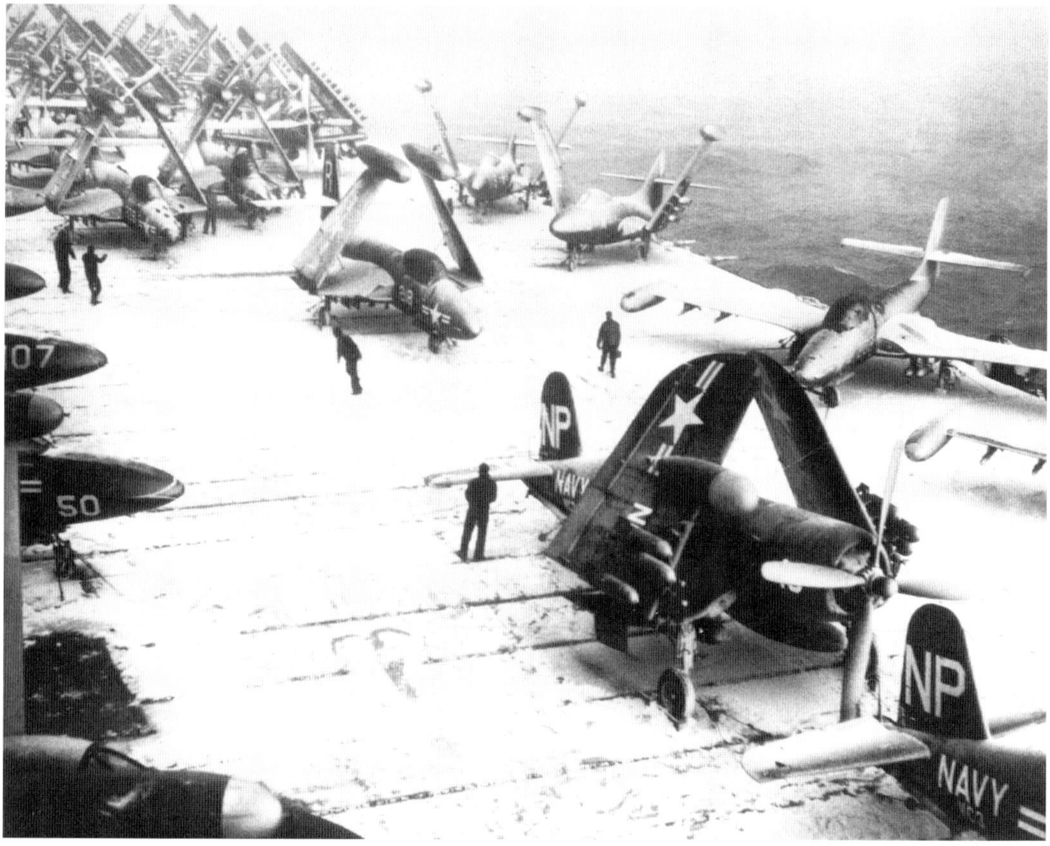
107
50
NP
NAVY
NP
NAVY

Above: The McDonnell F2H Banshee entered service in 1949 (as did the F9F Panther) and most pilots preferred it, particularly as its twin-engine configuration substantially improved the chances of survival in the event of combat damage. Although not as fast as the Panther, it had a higher service ceiling and greater range. However, it was larger and more expensive than the Grumman aircraft and consequently fewer were built. Nevertheless, Banshees played a prominent role in the Korean War and this F2H-2 of VF-172 is shown aboard USS *Essex* (CV-09) in August 1951. (NARA)

Opposite above: USS *Essex* leaving San Diego in June 1951 for the first of two deployments with Task Force 77 off Korea. On deck is an impressive array of aircraft from CVG-5, which included a squadron of F9F Panthers (VF-172), two squadrons of F4U Corsairs and a squadron of AD Skyraider attack aircraft. (NARA)

Opposite below: The Korean winter of 1951–2 was particularly severe and posed severe problems for the navy aircrews trying to support the hard-pressed UN troops ashore. Here snow covers the deck of USS *Essex* and parked aircraft, which include F2H Banshees, F9F Panthers, AD Skyraiders and F4U Corsairs, the latter flown by a detachment of Composite Squadron VC-3. (NARA)

Above: The last of twenty-four Essex class carriers to be commissioned was the USS *Oriskany* (CV-34), which was launched on 13 October 1945. However, work on her was suspended in August 1946 and restarted twelve months later. This delay was so that she could be rebuilt to SCB-27A standards and in this form she finally commissioned on 25 September 1950, and is shown here running trials around that time. Note the HO3S-1 helicopter on the fore deck. (NARA)

Opposite: The tracks of the two new H8 catapults fitted under SCB-27A are visible in this head-on view of USS *Oriskany*. The lighter coloured patches at the rear end of the tracks are the blast screens which could be raised and lowered hydraulically as required. (NARA)

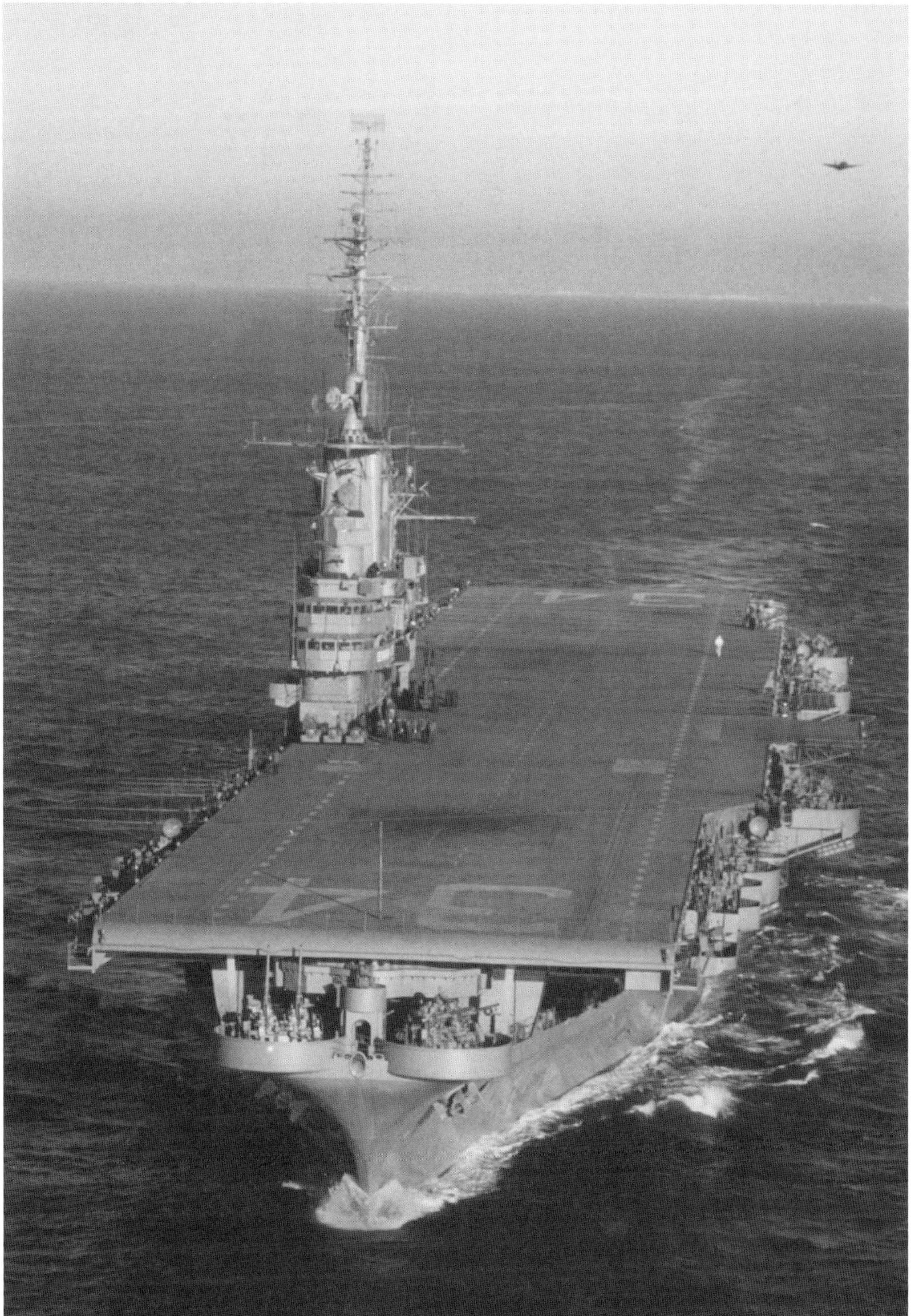

A Panther of VF-721 based aboard USS Boxer (CV-21) flies over north-east Korea near the Chosen reservoir in June 1951. The Grumman F9F Panther was the standard US Navy jet fighter during the Korean War and most Essex class carriers involved carried one or two squadrons. They were mainly used as escorts for prop-driven aircraft such as the Corsair and Skyraider and provided top cover during the strikes. However, operating the jets off the carriers with their axial flight decks was fraught with hazard and in light wind conditions they could not be launched carrying any ordnance apart from ammunition for the four 20mm cannon. (NARA)

Chapter Seven

Steam and Mirrors

The decade between the end of the Korean War and the start of involvement in Vietnam was a period of great change for the US Navy in general, and for the Essex class carriers in particular. The carriers were now required to accommodate and operate a new generation of swept-wing, and eventually supersonic, jet fighters and attack aircraft which were heavier, larger and thirstier than their predecessors. The earlier SCB-27A modifications had allowed the carriers to operate the first-generation jet fighters such as the Panther and Banshee, although even then the margins were critical. Consequently, a further upgrade designated SCB-27C was applied to a varied extent to six ships between 1951 and 1954. Most of the improvements brought in under SCB-27A were incorporated but with two significant additions. The previous hydraulic catapults were replaced by much more powerful steam catapults and the after aircraft lift was replaced by a larger deck-edge lift sited immediately behind the island superstructure. Other changes included a stronger arrester wire system to cope with heavier aircraft with higher landing speeds and waterline beam was increased to 103ft by the addition of bulges to improve stability.

The steam catapult was a British invention which was quickly adopted by the US Navy after HMS *Perseus*, fitted with a prototype system, visited the US in 1952 for demonstration and trials. This solved the problems associated with accelerating heavier aircraft to greater speeds, but landings were still a major cause of accidents. If an aircraft missed the arrester wires, it would at least be damaged in an engagement with the safety barrier, but in many cases would over run into the forward deck park causing serious damage and injury. The solution to this was another British innovation – the angled deck, or canted deck as the Americans initially called it. In 1952 the Essex class carrier *Antietam* was modified by the addition of an angled deck with its centreline offset by 10 degrees from ship's axis. Trials proved the system which revolutionised flight-deck operations and substantially reduced accident rates. Even before the trials were completed other carriers were being reconstructed along similar lines under a scheme designated SCB-125. As well as the angled deck, this also included the fitting of a so-called 'hurricane bow' to reduce the risk of damage in heavy weather conditions, improved arrester wire system with fewer wires, enlarging the forward lift, new flying control position on the side of the island and numerous detailed internal upgrades such as air conditioning in some areas. However, not all SCB-125 refits included the installation of steam catapults.

The first ship to complete the SCB-125 process (in 1954) was the USS *Shangri-La* (CVA-38), but in all fourteen Essex class were similarly modified between 1954 and 1959, most of which had already received either the SCB-27A or 27C upgrades. These changes were also contemporary with a change of role for some of the ships. Those that did not receive steam catapults were unable to operate the heavier

The US Navy's first operational swept-wing jet fighter was the Grumman F9F-6 Cougar, which was based on the straight-wing Panther. The first squadron formed in late 1952, too late to see action in the Korean War, although it subsequently saw widespread use and a total of 1,985 were delivered. However, the operation of the new generation of jets from the existing carriers was fraught with hazard but fortunately new inventions and techniques were just becoming available which would solve many of the issues. This Cougar flown by VF-61 is shown aboard USS *Intrepid* (CVA-11) in April 1956. (NARA)

attack aircraft and were designated as anti-submarine support carriers (CVS). This group was still known as the Essex class and also included others that retained the original axial flight deck. Those with both steam catapults and angled decks remained as attack carriers (CVA) and were officially known as the Ticonderoga class. Finally, in 1959–61, three ships (*Boxer*, *Princeton*, *Valley Forge*), all of which retained the axial flight deck, were modified to act as amphibious assault ships (LPH) and equipped with troop-carrying helicopters.

The third British invention which contributed substantially to the safe operation of aircraft was the Deck Landing Mirror Sight (DLMS), which was eventually fitted to all the carriers on a platform mounted on the port edge of the flight deck abreast the touchdown point and replaced the previous system of signal bats wielded by the Landing Deck Officer (LDO). Thus, in the decade following the Korean War the fleet of Essex class carriers were extensively modernised so that by the time of the Vietnam War they were able to continue as front-line assets in the US Navy.

The US Navy was quick to see the potential offered by the British idea of an angled flight deck and in 1952 selected the USS *Antietam* (CV-36) to be converted to test the concept. The work was carried out at New York Naval Shipyard between September and December 1952 and almost immediately trials with representative US Navy aircraft were initiated. This aerial view taken in January 1953 shows a selection of aircraft on deck, including Panthers and Banshees but also prototypes of the Navy's new generation of swept-wing fighters, the F9F-6 Cougar and the FJ-2 Fury. (NARA)

120

Opposite above: This aerial bow view of *Antietam* as converted to incorporate an angled flight deck gives a good idea of the flexibility offered by such an arrangement. With landing aircraft using the angled deck and, if necessary, having space to go around if they miss the wires, the forward flight deck is available for parking aircraft and others can be launched by catapult at the same time. The Gearing class destroyer USS *Corry* (DD817) is alongside. (NARA)

Opposite below: A busy flight-deck scene aboard USS *Antietam*, again illustrating the flexibility of the angled deck. In the foreground an F9F Panther is being prepared for launching from the port bow catapult while an AD Skyraider is making a conventional rolling take-off from the angled deck. A second Skyraider is in the background preparing to take off in turn. At this stage *Antietam* was still equipped with H-8 hydraulic catapults. (NARA)

In the summer of 1953 the USS *Antietam* sailed to Portsmouth, UK, to allow the Royal Navy to try out the angled deck concept (which, of course, was a British idea in the first place). For this purpose a number of Hawker Seahawks (806 NAS) and Supermarine Attackers embarked for a few days. The Attacker was the UK's first operational naval jet fighter and although obsolescent by 1953, it attracted considerable interest from the crew aboard *Antietam* by virtue of its unique tailwheel configuration. This example is being prepared for launching from the starboard catapult. (NARA)

Despite the success of the angled deck trials, it took time for this and other improvements to be incorporated in other carriers. This is USS *Philippine Sea* (CV-47) which, in 1954, was with the US Seventh Fleet based at Subic Bay in the Philippines. On deck can be seen aircraft of CVG-5, including not only Skyraiders and Panthers, but a squadron of the new swept-wing Grumman F9F-6 Cougar jet fighter. Despite operating this latest hot jet, the carrier still retains an axial flight deck and hydraulic catapults. In fact, *Philippine Sea* was one of five Essex class carriers which were not substantially altered or modernised throughout their careers. (NARA)

In the 1950s guided missiles began to be a practical proposition and one such was the XSSM-8 Regulus. Initially designed to be launched from surfaced submarines, it carried a 3,000lb warhead for up to 500 miles and was first tested in 1951. Later that year a second test was conducted from the USS *Princeton* (CV-37) and the missile entered limited service in 1954. Here a Regulus I is being prepared for firing as a training exercise from a mobile launcher aboard USS *Hancock* (CV-19) off the coast of California near NAS North Island. (NHHC)

The Regulus missile streaks away after a successful launch from USS *Hancock*. As well as submarines, some surface vessels were also equipped to carry and store the missile including the Essex class carriers *Lexington*, *Princeton* and *Randolph*, as well as *Hancock*. A later experimental development was the Regulus Assault Missile in which the missile was converted into an unmanned aerial vehicle which could be controlled and flown by remote control from a carrier-based aircraft and other Essex class were involved in these trials. However, the concept of the carriers acting as missile ships did not last long in view of the improved performance and capabilities of the new generation of naval jet aircraft. (NHHC)

Above: The first Essex class carrier to receive the full SCB-125 rebuild was USS *Shangri-La* (CV-38). In November 1952 she entered the Puget Sound Naval Shipyard and when she emerged two years later she was almost a new ship. The most obvious change was the new angled flight deck, but she was also equipped with a pair of powerful steam catapults. Also visible is a new deck-edge elevator on the starboard side aft of the island superstructure which replaced the previous after elevator positioned on the centreline of the old axial flight deck. This arrangement allowed movement of aircraft to and from the hangar without disrupting flight operations. Note also the platform running around the base of the starboard side of the island which assisted the movement and parking of vehicles without obstructing flight-deck movements. (NARA)

Opposite above: Shangri-La's modernisation also included the SCB-27C improvements. This view of her after completing her modernisation refit shows the tapering guidelines painted on the angle deck which gave a better visual reference to pilots of landing aircraft. Compared with the trial installation on USS *Antietam*, the overhang of the angled deck is increased in area. Also, on ships with the angled deck the number of arrester wires was reduced from thirteen to eight as any aircraft that missed the wires could safely go around and make another approach. (NARA)

Ooposite below: Covered in scaffolding and work shelters, USS *Yorktown* (now CVA-10) undergoes the SCB-125 modernisation at Puget Sound Naval Shipyard. As she had already undergone the SCB-27A refit, the further upgrade work was effected in a relatively short period between March and November 1955. (NHHC)

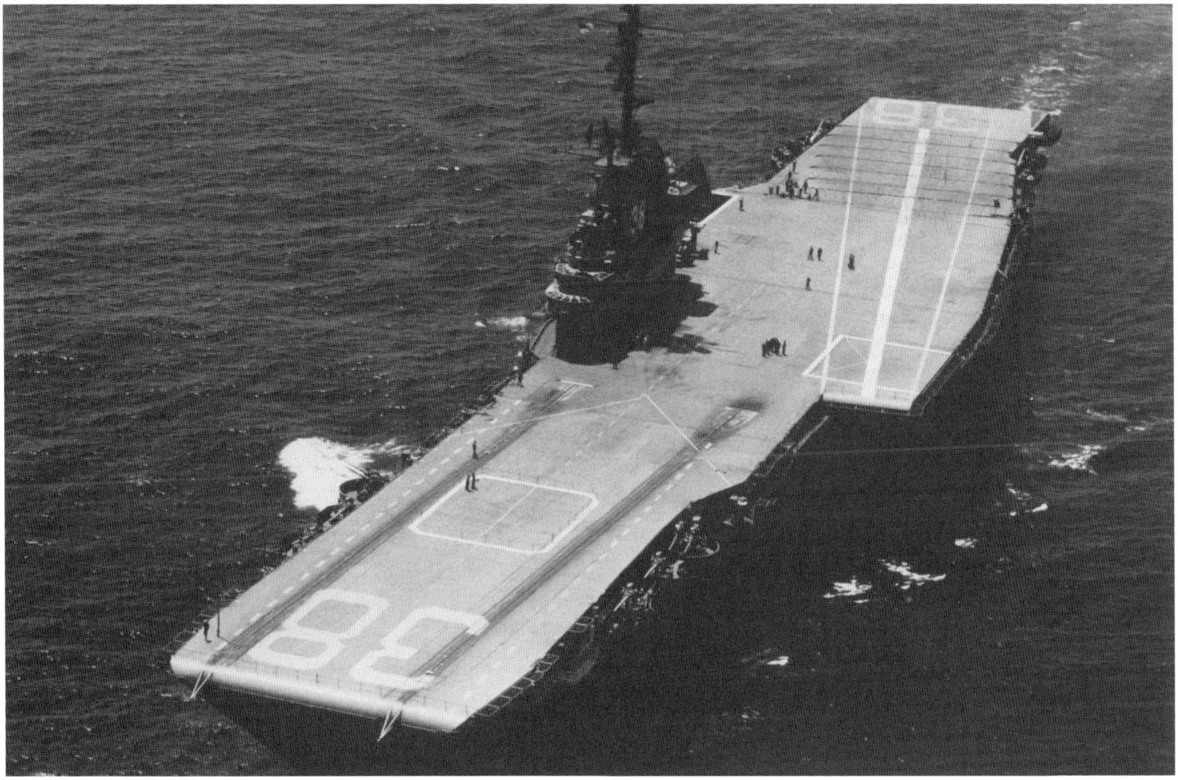

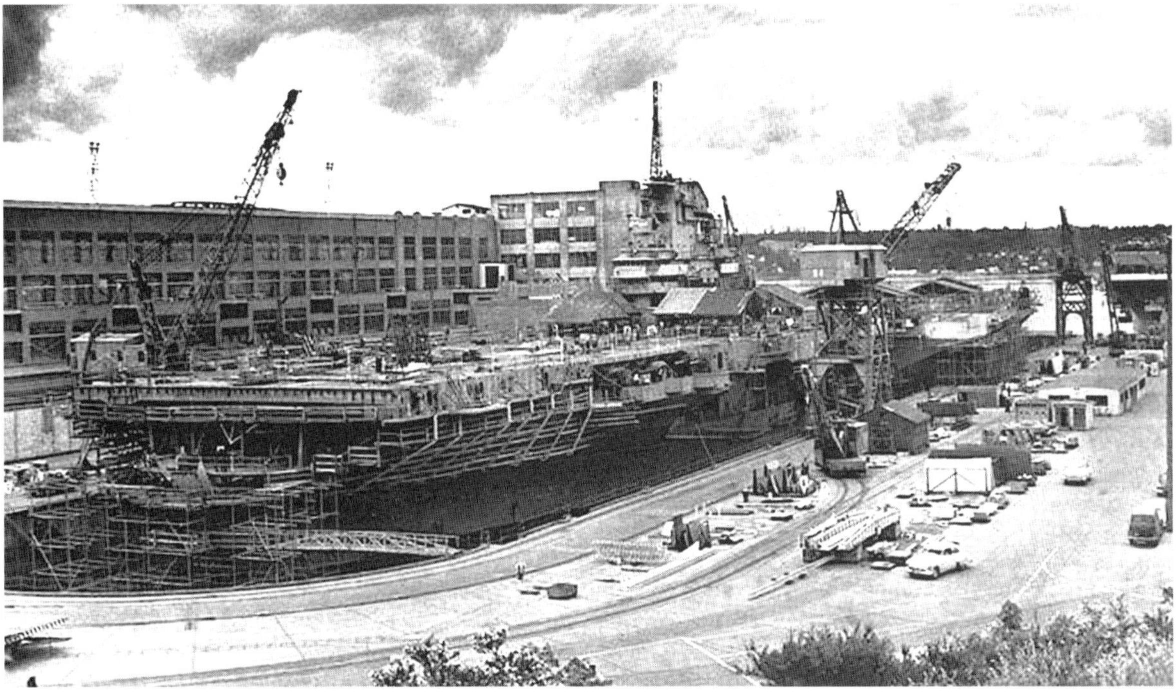

126

Above: Having already undergone an SCB-27A modernisation refit in 1949–51, the SCB-125 upgrade for USS *Essex* (CVA-9) was achieved between July 1955 and March 1956 at the Puget Sound Naval Shipyard. She is shown here later in 1956 with aircraft of CVG-2 embarked, including F9F-6 Cougars, F2H Banshees and, right aft, a pair of AD-4W Skyraider AEW aircraft. In 1955 the US Navy adopted a standard aircraft camouflage scheme of light-grey upper surfaces and white undersides which replaced the overall midnight-blue scheme which had been introduced in 1944. For the next few years it was not uncommon to see a mix of the old and new colour schemes, as illustrated here. (NARA)

Opposite above: USS *Lexington* (CVA-16 after September 1952) was one of three Essex class carriers which received the SCB-27 and SCB-125 modernisations in a single refit. In this case she entered the Puget Sound Naval Shipyard in September 1953 and recommissioned almost two years later on 15 August 1955 (coincidently exactly ten years after the formal end of the war in the Pacific). This view of her on completion shows the so-called 'hurricane bow' which was incorporated in all the SCB-125 conversions and was similar to the bow profile of wartime British aircraft carriers. The original Essex class design with bow-mounted AA guns and an overhanging flight deck had proved prone to storm damage (see image of USS *Hornet* on p. 85). (NARA)

Opposite below: After two deployments in the Korean War, USS *Bon Homme Richard* (now CVA-31) became the third carrier to receive the combined SCB-27C/SCB-125 refit and this work was carried out in the San Francisco Naval Shipyard between May 1953 and October 1955. She is shown here in January 1956 while carrying out post-refit trials. Note that the starboard deck-edge elevator is stowed in the upright position. (NARA)

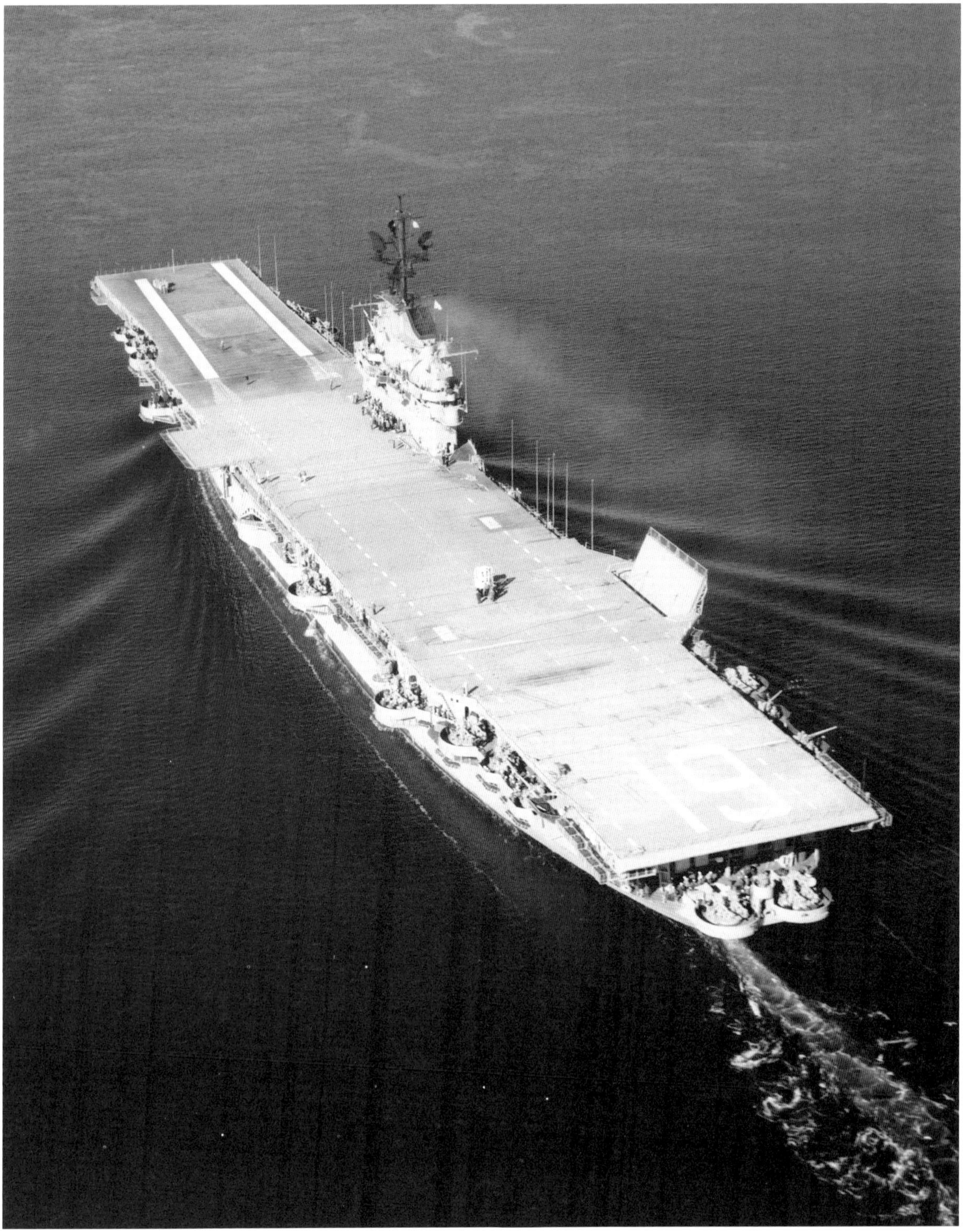
19

Opposite: The first Essex class carrier to undergo the SCB-27C modernisation was USS *Hancock* (CVA-19), the work being carried out between December 1951 and February 1954. This view shows the ship just after completion of the refit which included the addition of an after-deck edge lift and a strengthened flight deck, the lighter shaded area showing the extent of such work. The most significant addition was the installation of a pair of C-11 steam catapults, the first such installation in the US Navy. (NHHC)

Following her refit and after initial sea trials, the USS *Hancock* proceeded to carry out a series of tests with the new steam catapults. On 1 June 1954 a Grumman S2F-1 Tracker ASW aircraft flown by Commander Henry J. Jackson USN was the first aircraft to be launched from a US carrier by means of a steam catapult. This was a good test of the new system as at a maximum take-off weight of almost 27,000lb the Tracker was considerably heavier than, for example, the F9F Panther at less than 19,000lb. At the time the Tracker had only just entered service with VS-26 but would go on to be the US Navy's main ASW aircraft until replaced by the jet-powered S-3 Viking from 1974 onwards. (NHHC)

Above: Immediately after the Second World War the US Navy was determined to play a major role in the new atomic age and ordered a large carrier-based bomber which would be able to carry and deliver a nuclear weapon. The result was the North American AJ Savage which entered service in 1949, although at that time the only carriers fully capable of operating the aircraft were the three large Midway class. However, Savage detachments were occasionally embarked on Essex class carriers for short periods, including this example flown by VC-7 (Composite Squadron) aboard USS *Wasp* (CVA-18) during the latter's 1953–4 world cruise. (NHHC)

Opposite above: The SCB-125 modernisation programme, which included the provision of an angled and strengthened flight deck, allowed the Savage to operate more regularly from the relevant Essex class, although even then the size of the aircraft caused difficulties. This view of an AJ-2 Savage of VAH-6 landing aboard USS *Bennington* (CVA-20) during a 1956–7 Pacific deployment gives some idea of the great size of this bomber which featured a jet engine in the tail in addition to the two radial piston engines. (NHHC)

Opposite below: The US Navy's desire to possess a nuclear-capable bomber eventually resulted in production of the Douglas A3D Skywarrior. This was an advanced swept-wing twin jet, considerably larger and heavier than any previous carrier-based naval aircraft. The prototype flew as early as October 1952, but engine development issues delayed an initial entry into service with VAH-1 until March 1956. The squadron subsequently embarked on USS *Shangri-La* (CVA-38) for operational trials and here one of the Skywarriors has just been launched with another being readied. Without the introduction of the C-11 steam catapult, the operation of an aircraft of this size would not have been possible. (NHHC)

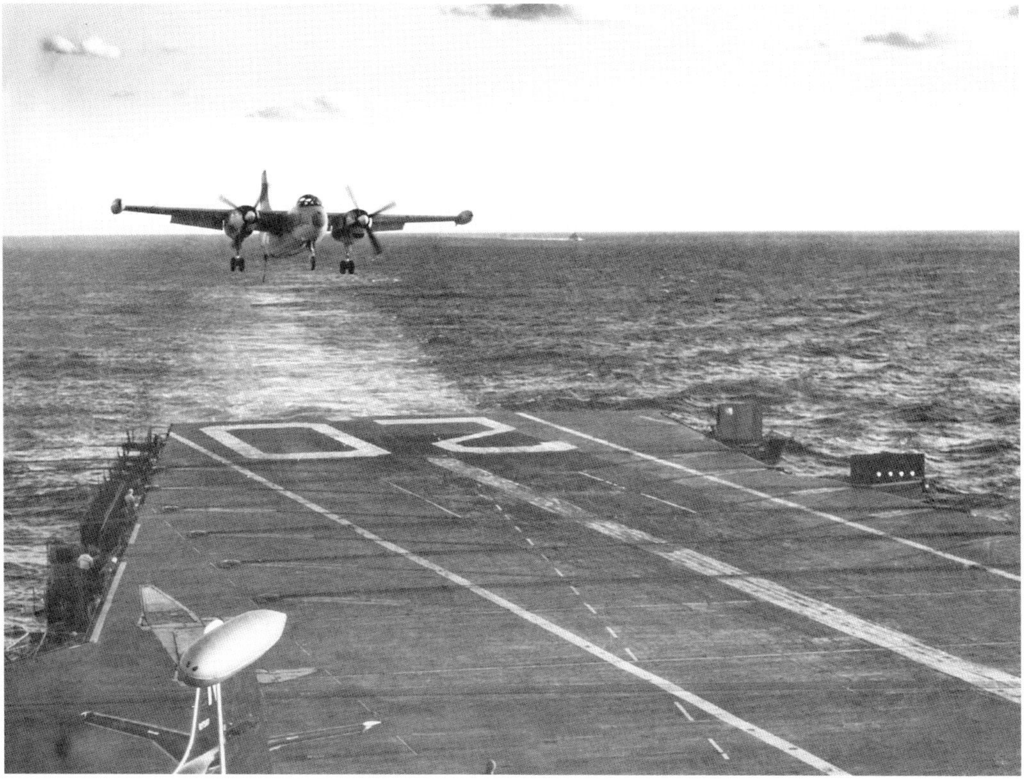

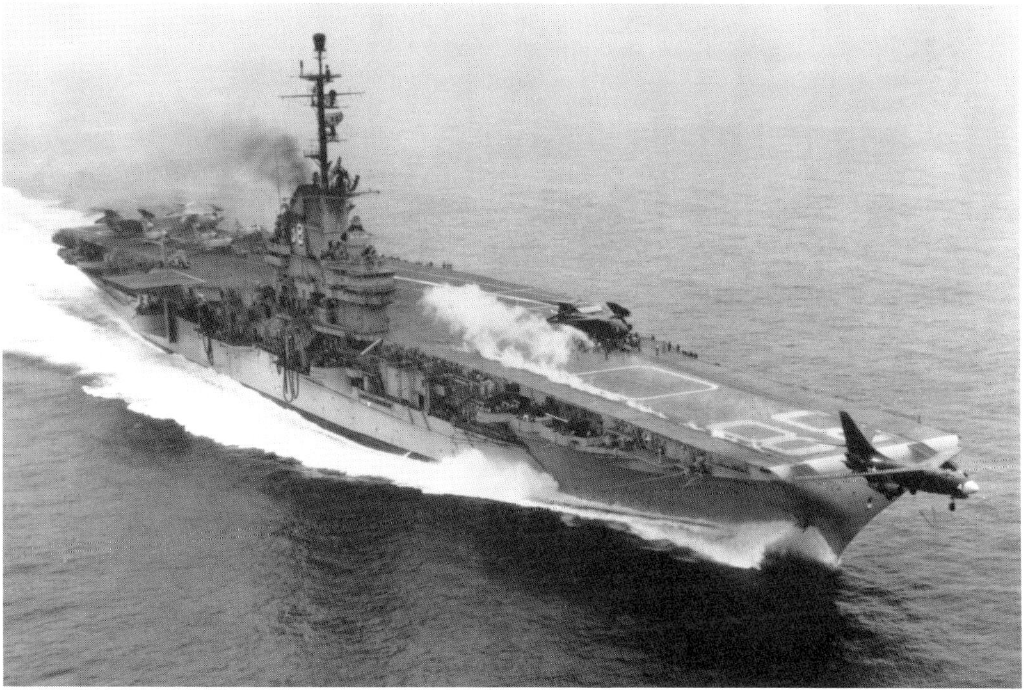

Above: The threat to carrier task forces posed by the new generation of Soviet jet bombers such as the Tupolev Tu-16 (Badger) lead to a requirement for a fast-climbing, deck-launched fighter which could intercept the bombers before they could reach a weapon-release point. The outcome was the Douglas F4D Skyray, which was also the first US Navy fighter capable of exceeding Mach 1.0 in level flight. First flown in 1951, engine issues delayed service introduction until 1956, although it subsequently served with eleven front-line squadrons. This Skyray served with VF-23 as part of CVG-15 aboard the USS *Hancock* (CVA-19) from February to October 1958. (NARA)

Opposite: Apart from the steam catapult and angled deck, the other British innovation which was quickly adopted by the US Navy was the mirror landing sight. This trial installation was placed on the flight deck abaft the island aboard USS *Randolph* (CVA-15) in 1955. Out of the picture to the left would be a spotlight directed at the mirror and this would appear in the mirror as a bright ball, colloquially known as the 'meatball', to the pilot of an approaching aircraft (in this case an AD Skyraider whose reflection can be seen). The position of the meatball relative to the horizontal side-bar lights would indicate to the pilot his position relative to the optimum approach path. (US Navy)

133

I
6415
NAVY
VF-41
105

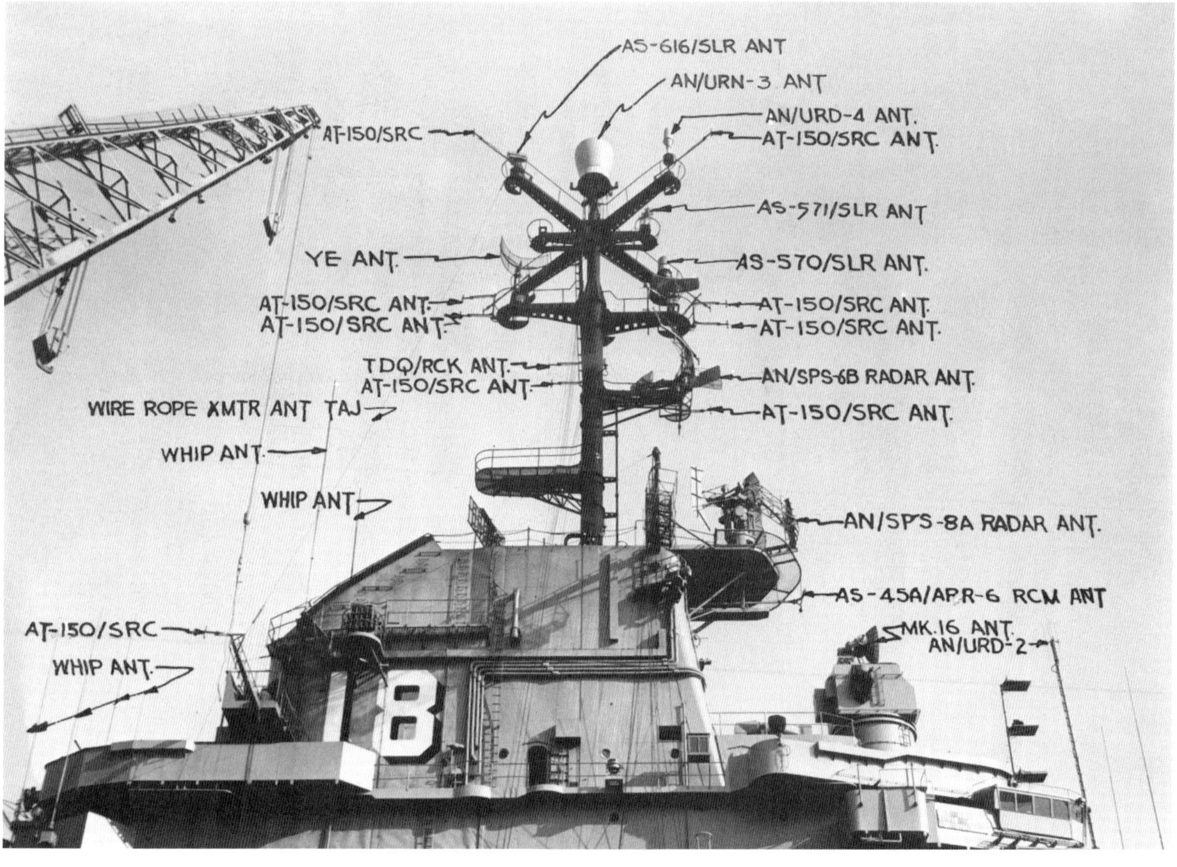
AS-616/SLR ANT
AN/URN-3 ANT
AN/URD-4 ANT.
AT-150/SRC
AT-150/SRC ANT.
AS-571/SLR ANT
YE ANT.
AS-570/SLR ANT.
AT-150/SRC ANT.
AT-150/SRC ANT.
AT-150/SRC ANT.
AT-150/SRC ANT.
TDQ/RCK ANT.
AT-150/SRC ANT.
AN/SPS-6B RADAR ANT.
WIRE ROPE XMTR ANT TAJ
AT-150/SRC ANT.
WHIP ANT.
WHIP ANT.
AN/SPS-8A RADAR ANT.
AS-45A/APR-6 RCM ANT
AT-150/SRC
MK.16 ANT.
AN/URD-2
WHIP ANT.
18

Opposite above: An F2H-3 Banshee of VF-41 (Black Aces) taxis forward after landing aboard USS *Bennington* (CVA-20) in October 1956 as the ship was preparing for a Pacific deployment. In the background can be seen the mirror deck-landing sight mounted on a platform projecting from the port side of the flight deck, this being the standard position for all subsequent installations. In fact, the ship had just completed a successful fleet evaluation of the combination of an angled deck and mirror landing sight which would subsequently provide a 75 per cent reduction in deck-landing accidents. (NMNA)

Opposite below: As well as improving facilities for the operation of aircraft, the various SCB modernisation schemes incorporated an ever-increasing array of radars and other electronic equipment, as illustrated by this captioned photograph of USS *Wasp* (CVA-18) in 1955 on completion of her SCB-125 refit. Compare with the photograph on p. 56 of the wartime radars aboard USS *Hornet* (CV-12). (NARA)

The US Navy's second swept-wing fighter to enter service was the North American FJ-2/3 Fury, which was basically a naval version of Air Force's F-86 Sabre which had performed so well in Korea. This example is an FJ-3M belonging to VF-211 preparing to launch from USS *Bon Homme Richard* (CVA-31) in June 1956. The 'M' suffix indicates that this version of the Fury is equipped to carry AAM-N-7/AIM-9A Sidewinder missiles, a pair of these being carried on the inboard underwing pylons. (NARA)

In late 1956 the *Bon Homme Richard* was also host to another of the Navy's swept-wing jet fighters – the unconventional tailless Vought F7U-3 Cutlass. VF-211 was equipped with the F7U-3M Cutlass which carried Sparrow air-to-air missiles, and one of their aircraft is landing aboard in August 1956. The squadron formed part of the ship's air group until February 1957. However, the Cutlass proved to have an appalling accident record, the worst of any Navy jet fighter, and consequently was withdrawn from front-line service at the end of 1957. (NARA)

Chapter Eight

Submarines, Spacecraft and Vietnam

As mentioned in the previous chapter, several Essex class were modified to act in the anti-submarine role. For this purpose they carried an air group which normally comprised two squadrons equipped with a total of twenty-four S2F (S-2) Tracker ASW aircraft, one squadron of sixteen HSS (HS-34) or HS-3 Sea King helicopters and detachments of specialised aircraft for the photo reconnaissance (RF-8 Crusaders) and AEW (EA-1 Skyraiders) roles. In addition, there were three A-4 Skyhawks for self-defence, making a total of about forty-nine/fifty aircraft. In an era when the Soviet submarine threat was at its highest, the Essex class CVS played an important role.

Another task which fell to the Essex class, and could scarcely have been foreseen at the time of their inception, was to act as command ships for the location and recovering of various spacecraft and their astronauts. This began in 1961 with the recovery of the first American in space, Alan Shepard, and his Freedom 7 capsule. This was part of the Mercury space programme and was followed by the two-man Gemini series which in turn led to the Apollo programme and men landing on the moon. Almost all of these missions were recovered to Essex class carriers, including the Apollo 11 crew returning from their momentous moon landing mission in 1969.

By that time the US Navy was heavily involved in the Vietnam War, which raged through most of the 1960s and into the following decade. Despite a temporary halt in attacks against North Vietnam in 1974–5, US carriers were still involved in supporting US forces that remained deployed in South Vietnam, which eventually was overrun by communist forces in 1975. In all nine Essex/Ticonderoga class carriers were involved in Vietnam operations between 1964 and 1973. Most of these acted in the CVS role but *Hancock* (CVA-19) and *Ticonderoga* (CVA-14) continued as front-line attack carriers, while *Intrepid* (CVS-11) and *Shangri-La* (CVS-38) were at times utilised as limited capability attack carriers. Their air groups were equipped with F-8 Crusaders and A-4 Skyhawks as opposed to the larger

Above: In 1956 the first of the new breed of 60,000-ton super carriers (USS *Forrestal* (CVA-59)) entered service and by the end of the decade three more were in commission. By that time many Essex class carriers were no longer required in the attack role and were re-tasked as ASW Support carriers (CVS). Surprisingly, this included several of the most recently completed ships including USS *Leyte*, which was restyled CVS-32 in 1953 after minimal modifications and recommissioned in January 1954. This later view (*c*. 1957) shows her with an ASW air group embarked, which included Sikorsky HO4S helicopters, Grumman S2F Trackers and Douglas AD-4W Skyraiders. (NMNA)

Midway and Forrestal classes which carried F-4 Phantoms, A-6 Intruders and A-7 Corsair IIs.

Vietnam was the swansong for the Essex class carriers. Most of those which had not been involved in the Vietnam War had been decommissioned or laid up by 1970, while the rest were quickly decommissioned by 1976, except for the USS *Lexington* (see Chapter Nine).

Opposite below: As an attack carrier, USS *Randolph* (CVA-15) underwent the SCB-27A modernisation in 1951–2 and the SCB-125 rebuild, adding the angled deck, in 1955–6. However, she was reclassified as an ASW carrier (CVS-15) in March 1959 and this photo shows her acting that role later in the year. Ranged on deck are the S2F-1 Trackers of VS-36, a pair of AD-5W AEW Skyraiders and several HSS-1 Seabat helicopters. (NHHC)

Above: The principal equipment of ASW air groups was the Grumman S2F Tracker (re-designated S-2 after 1962). It first flew in December 1952 and was a dedicated anti-submarine aircraft equipped with a range of sensors and able to carry depth charges, torpedoes and rockets. This Tracker belonging to VS-25 is about to touch down on the recently modernised USS *Shangri-La* (CVA-36) during angled deck trials. (NARA)

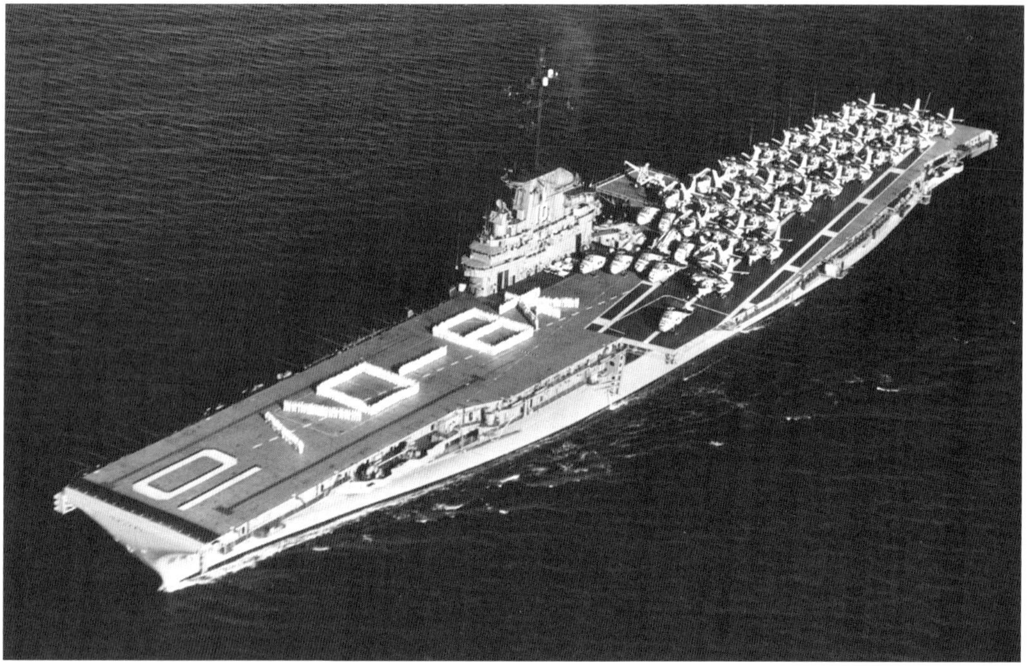
10

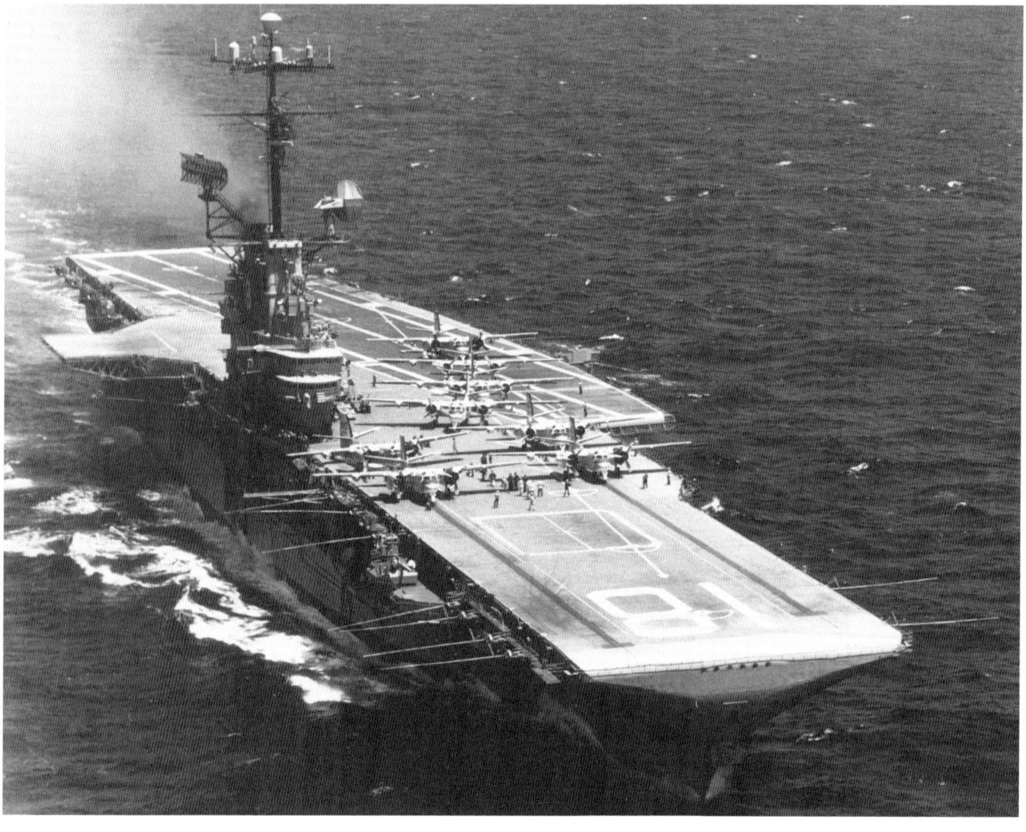
18

Opposite above: The USS *Yorktown* was re-classified as CVS-10 in 1957 and recommissioned in her new role in February 1958. In 1960 she was operating in the Far East and this aerial view shows her about to enter Yokosuka for a courtesy visit to the Japanese port. Her crew are arranged on deck to spell out 'Hello Japan' in Japanese characters. Ranged on deck are HSS-1N Seabat helicopters of HS-4 (Black Knights), S2F-1 Trackers of VS-23 (Black Cats) and a few AD-5W Skyraiders of VAW-11 (Early Eleven). (NHHC)

Opposite below: Some of the carriers allocated to the ASW Support role, such as *Leyte* (CVS-32), *Tarawa* (CVS-40) and *Philippine Sea* (CVS-47), underwent only minimal modifications and essentially retained the original axial flight deck layout. However, others which had undergone SCB-27C and SCB-125 updates were initially employed as attack carriers (CVA) and later re-deployed as ASW carriers (CVS). Among the latter was USS *Wasp* (CVS-18), shown here in 1967 with S-2 Trackers of Carrier Anti-Submarine Air Group 52 (CVSG-52) lining up for take-off with two of aircraft ready for launching from the steam catapults. (NHHC)

Several support carriers were deployed in support of Task Force 77 off Vietnam. This is USS *Bennington* (CVS-20) taking on ordnance and stores from the ammunition ship USS *Mauna Kae* (AE0-22) in the Gulf of Tonkin on 10 September 1968 during the last of three deployments between 1965 and November 1968. On deck are aircraft of CVSG-59, including S-2 Trackers and a couple of E-1B Tracer AEW aircraft, as well as SH-3 Sea King helicopters. (NHHC)

141

Above: The large SH-3 Sea King represented a substantial increase in effectiveness in the ASW role when compared with previous helicopters such as the HSS-1, which it replaced. The USS *Randolph* was converted to the CVS role in March 1959 and a Sea King of ASW helicopter squadron HS-3 can be seen lifting off from the deck in September 1965 with a line of Trackers ranged along the port side of the flight deck ready to take off in return. Noteworthy in this photo is that flight deck appears to be still faced with wood planking even after modernisations. (NMNA)

Opposite above: In the 1960s several of the Essex class support carriers came to be involved in the recovery of various astronauts and their space capsules – a task that would have been in the realms of science fiction at the time when these ships were first commissioned. The first of these missions was carried out by USS *Lake Champlain* on 5 May 1961 when helicopters from the ship picked up astronaut Alan Shepard in his capsule Freedom 7 after becoming the first American in space. He is shown on the ship's deck immediately after climbing out of the spacecraft. *Lake Champlain* was later involved in the recovery of the unmanned Gemini 2 and on 25 August 1965 recovered Gemini 5 and its two astronauts. Almost immediately afterwards she was laid up and then decommissioned in May 1966. (NASA)

Opposite below: On 16 December 1965 the USS *Wasp* (CVS-18) acted as recovery ship for the Gemini 6 capsule, which is seen here in the water while an SH-3 Sea King of HS-11 (Sub Seekers) approaches to recover the astronauts Schirra and Stafford. Gemini 6 had just completed an historic mission involving the first rendezvous in space with another space craft – Gemini 7, which was recovered two days later after spending a record fourteen days in space. *Wasp* was also involved in the recovery of Gemini 4, 9 and 12. (NASA)

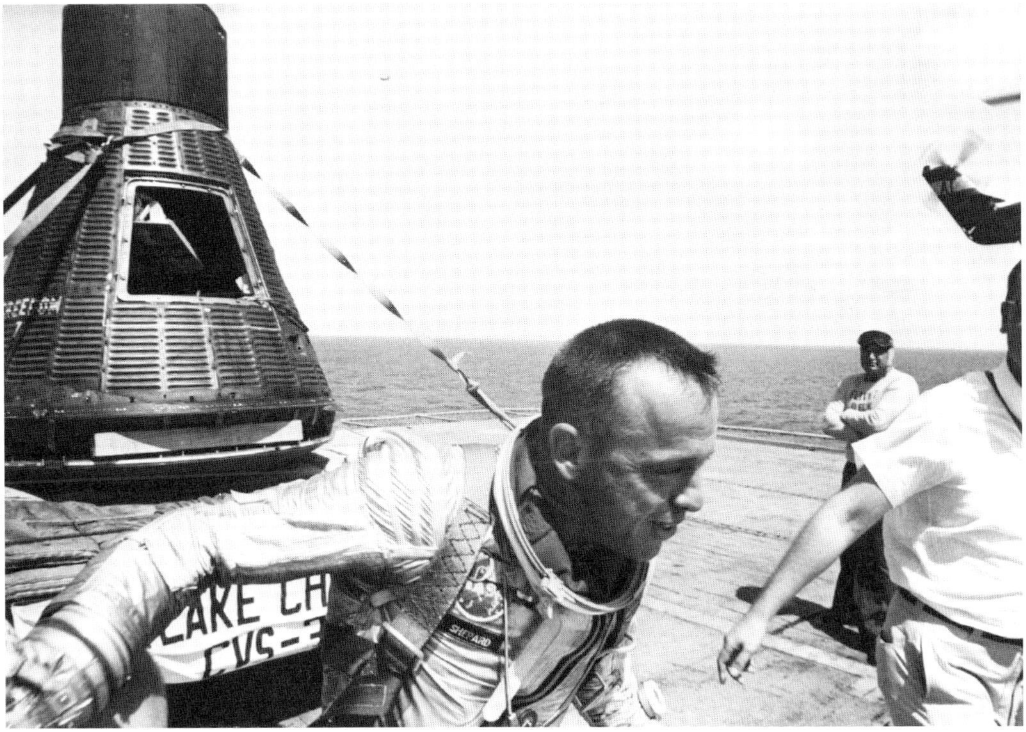
LAKE CH
SHEPARD

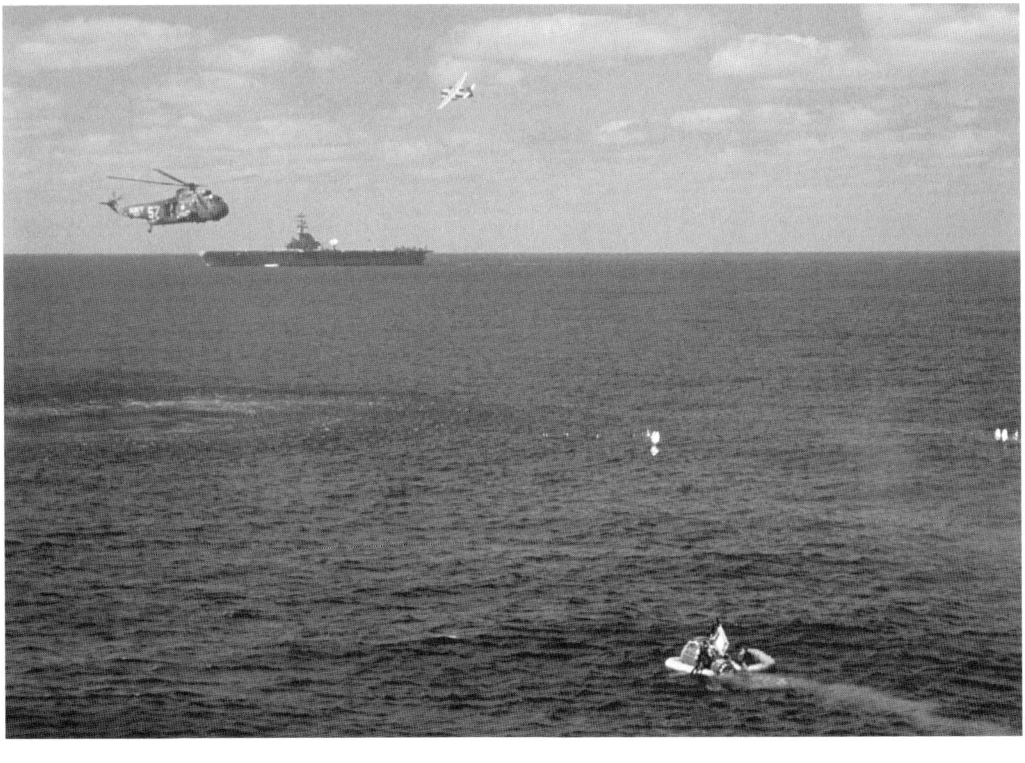

Above: The Gemini programme of twelve launches pioneered systems and techniques for the later Apollo missions which would culminate in men landing on the moon. However, this got off to a tragic start when the first manned mission, Apollo 3, blew up on the launch pad killing all three astronauts. The next three missions were therefore unmanned as various components of the Apollo spacecraft and its Saturn rocket were tested. The first of these was Apollo 4, which splashed down in the Pacific 1,075 miles north-west of Hawaii on 9 November 1967. USS *Bennington* (CVS-20) is here manoeuvring to recover the capsule. (NASA)

Opposite above: Apollo 10 was a dress rehearsal for a landing on the moon and the Lunar Excursion Module (LEM) was flown down to only 50,000ft above the moon's surface. The crew then returned to Earth in the Command Module (CM) and splashed down on 26 May 1969, when they were recovered by USS *Princeton* (LPH-5), which by that time had been re-assigned as an amphibious assault transport. This overhead view shows the unaltered outline of the flight deck now marked out with a dozen helicopter landing spots. The Apollo 10 CM capsule is being hoisted out by crane and is visible just forward of the deck-edge elevator. (NMNA)

Neil Armstrong was the first man to set foot on the moon and he and fellow astronauts Buzz Aldrin and Michael Collins were transported there by the Apollo 11 mission. On return the CM splashed down 900 miles south-west of Hawaii on 24 July 1969 and the crew were immediately transferred by helicopter to the recovery ship, USS *Hornet* (CVS-12), where they were greeted by President Nixon. *Hornet* is shown here subsequently manoeuvring to recover the empty capsule. The ship was also involved in the recovery of Apollo 12 in November 1969 but was finally decommissioned and laid up in June 1970. (NMNA)

Above: As the era of space exploration got underway the US Navy looked at how it might be possible to provide mobile ship-based launch pads. This would enable satellites to be launched into orbits that were not then accessible from fixed land-based launch sites. One proposal in 1961, illustrated here, was to convert an Essex class carrier by siting a gantry and launch pad for an Atlas rocket on the after section of the ship. However, such funding as was available was directed to the conventional launch sites and the idea progressed no further than a paper concept. (NHHC)

Opposite above: US Navy carriers became involved in the nascent Vietnam War on 2 August 1964 when the Destroyer USS *Maddox* (DD731) called for air support while being engaged by North Vietnam gunboats in the Gulf of Tonkin. The only carrier in the area was the USS *Ticonderoga* (CVA-14) and four of her F-8E Crusaders of VF-53 (Iron Angels) responded, sinking at least one of the gunboats and starting the shooting war which was to continue in one way or another until 1975. USS *Ticonderoga* is shown here in 1957 off Point Loma, San Diego, shortly after completing her SCB-125 modernisation refit. (NMNA)

Opposite below: Although classified as an ASW Support Carrier in 1962 and designated CVS-11, the USS *Intrepid* actually carried out three deployments to the Gulf of Tonkin as an Attack Carrier between 1966 and 1968. This image dates from 13 September 1966 during the first deployment with CVW-10 embarked. This included two squadrons of A-4B Skyhawks (VA-15 and VA-95) and two squadrons of A-1H Skyraiders (VA-165 and VA-176) and in fact one of the latter from VA-165 was lost that day after being hit by AAA fire over North Vietnam, although the pilot was recovered. (NHHC)

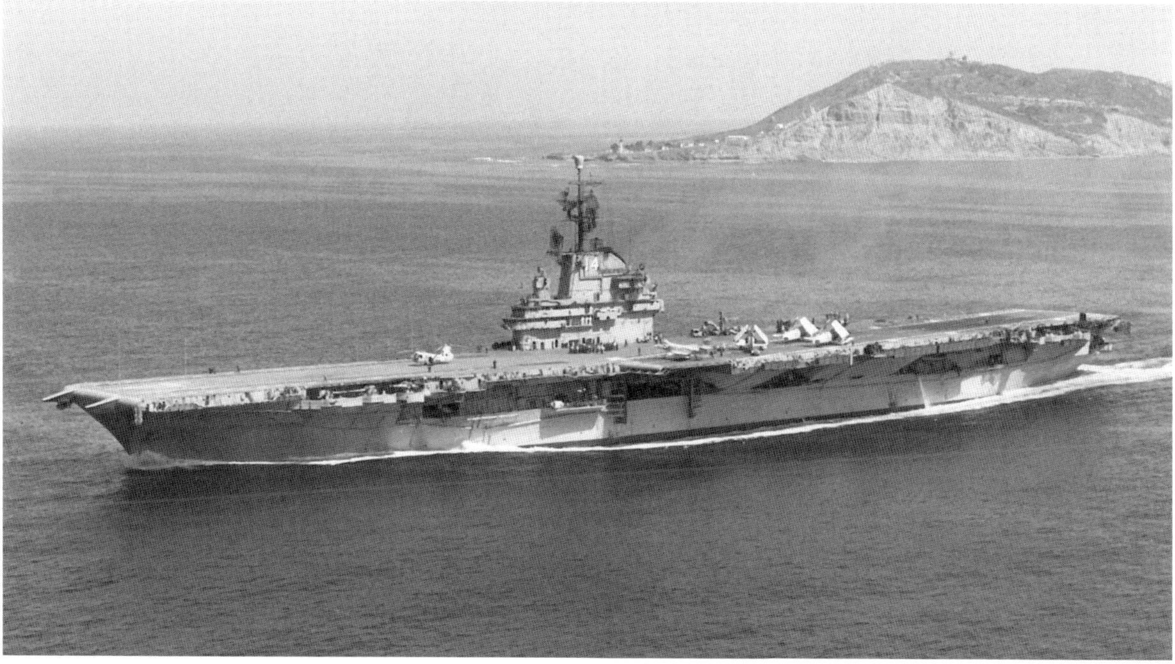

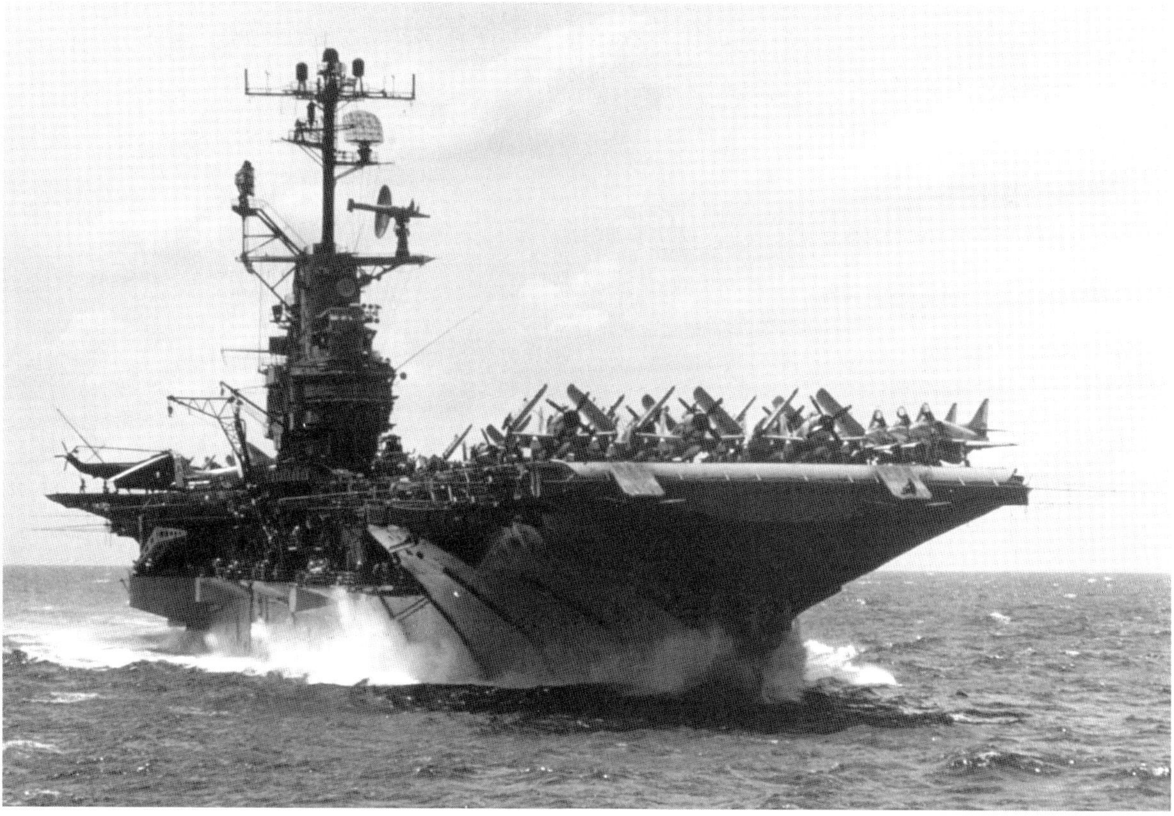

An A-4E Skyhawk belonging to VA-106 (Gladiators) is positioned onto one of *Intrepid*'s steam catapults as she prepares to launch a strike against North Vietnam in September 1968 during her final deployment. At that time CVW-10 included three squadrons of Skyhawks and two detachments of F-8 Crusaders, as well as a detachment of Grumman E-1 Tracer AEW aircraft. (NHHC)

In the era of supersonic jets the venerable piston-engined Skyraider still played a significant role in strikes against Viet Kong targets. Its great attributes were an ability to lift a significant load of ordnance and its long-range endurance, which allowed it to loiter for lengthy periods around a potential target area. This is an A-1H Skyraider of VA-215 (Barn Owls) preparing to take off from USS *Hancock* (CVA-19) for a raid on a North Vietnamese training base in February 1965. In the background are F-8 Crusaders of VF-24 and VF-211, which also formed part of the carrier's air wing (CVW-21). (NMNA)

The USS *Bon Homme Richard* (CVA-31) made no less than five deployments off Vietnam between January 1964 and October 1969. This photograph showing an A-4E Skyhawk of VA-94 over the ship as she cruises in the Gulf of Tonkin was taken in August 1969 during the ship's last deployment. (NHHC)

Left: No less than ten Essex class carriers were involved in the Vietnam War, although only six of those were fully modified to SCB-27C/SBC-125 standard to operate jet aircraft in the attack role; the remaining four were classified as ASW support carriers (CVS). The attack carriers operated with an air wing made up of five squadrons and various specialised detachments for a total of around seventy aircraft. Shown here in September 1969 is the USS *Hancock* (CVA-19) in the foreground, which was in the process of relieving the USS *Ticonderoga* sailing astern of her. Shortly afterwards *Ticonderoga* would have set course for her home port at Alameda CA, where she arrived on 18 September 1969. (NHHC)

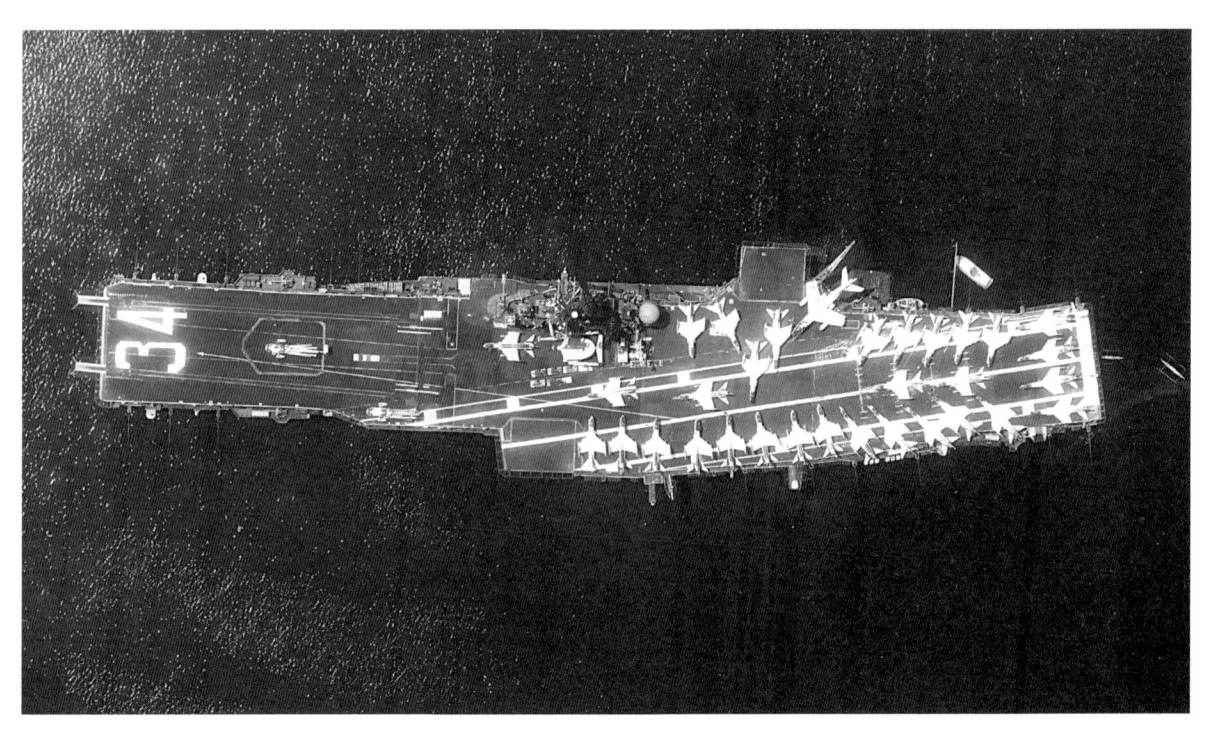

Above: USS *Bon Homme Richard* (CVA-31) underway in the Gulf of Tonkin on 13 June 1969 during her penultimate Vietnam deployment. On deck are a variety of aircraft, including F-8J Crusaders of VF-51 and 53, A-4F Skyhawks of VA-22 and 144, and behind the island and on the port catapult are two EKA-3B Skywarriors. The latter's roles included air-to-air refuelling and EW/ECM duties. The ship's radars include an SPS-30 air search radar with height-finding capability with its characteristic parabolic reflector antenna, and an SPS-43 long-range search radar with its 'bedstead' antenna mounted beside the funnel. The dome on the after edge of the island houses the CCA (carrier controlled approach) radar. (NHHC)

Opposite below: One of the last Essex class to be involved in Vietnam operations was USS *Oriskany* (CVA-34), which participated in the final series of strikes against Viet Kong positions right up to the signing of the Paris Peace Accord on 27 January 1973. Even then her air wing CVW-19 conducted further attacks against communist forces in Laos during February before finally withdrawing to Subic Bay in the Philippines. This overhead view shows the ship in 1974 during her penultimate deployment with the Seventh Fleet and gives an excellent impression of the deck layout of SCB-125 ships. On deck F-8 Crusaders and A-7E Corsair IIs, the latter of which by then had replaced the older A-4 Skyhawk in front-line service. *Oriskany* was finally decommissioned in April 1976. (NMNA)

Above: Another long-lived Essex class was USS *Hancock* (CVA-19), which was in action off Vietnam until the very end of 1973. This photo shows her at San Diego in February 1975 but by April she was again approaching Vietnam. By this time her air wing had been replaced by Marine helicopter units which were involved in the evacuation of US personnel and their families from Phnom Penh in Cambodia and from Saigon at the end of April as North Vietnam forces overran the city, effectively ending US involvement in the Vietnam War. Subsequently, *Hancock* was decommissioned on 30 January 1976 after a career spanning almost thirty-two years. (NMNA)

Opposite above: After an active involvement in the Korean War the USS *Boxer* was redesignated as an ASW support carrier (CVS-21). However, in 1957–8 the ship was engaged in trials to test the concept of amphibious assault operations using helicopters. As a result, she was permanently modified for this role and reclassified as a Landing Platform (Helicopter), redesignated LPH-4 and is shown here in 1964. During the Vietnam War she was employed as an aircraft transport, carrying 200 helicopters for the 1st Air Cavalry Division and on another occasion replacement aircraft for Marine air squadrons. However, she was not involved in any combat missions and was subsequently decommissioned on 1 December 1969. (NHHC)

Opposite below: Like *Boxer*, USS *Princeton* was also designated as an ASW support carrier (CVS-37) in 1954, and subsequently converted to an amphibious assault carrier (LPH-5) in 1959. The modifications included removal of equipment required for fixed wing operations (e.g. arrester wires and catapults) and converting sections of the hangar deck into accommodation for a battalion-sized Marine unit (approximately 650 men). Two of the twin 5in gun mountings were removed together with all the close-range 40mm weapons. The ship was extensively involved in several assault and support missions during the Vietnam War, in all making four deployments to the war zone as part of the Amphibious Ready Group. She finally decommissioned on 30 January 1970. (NMNA)

152

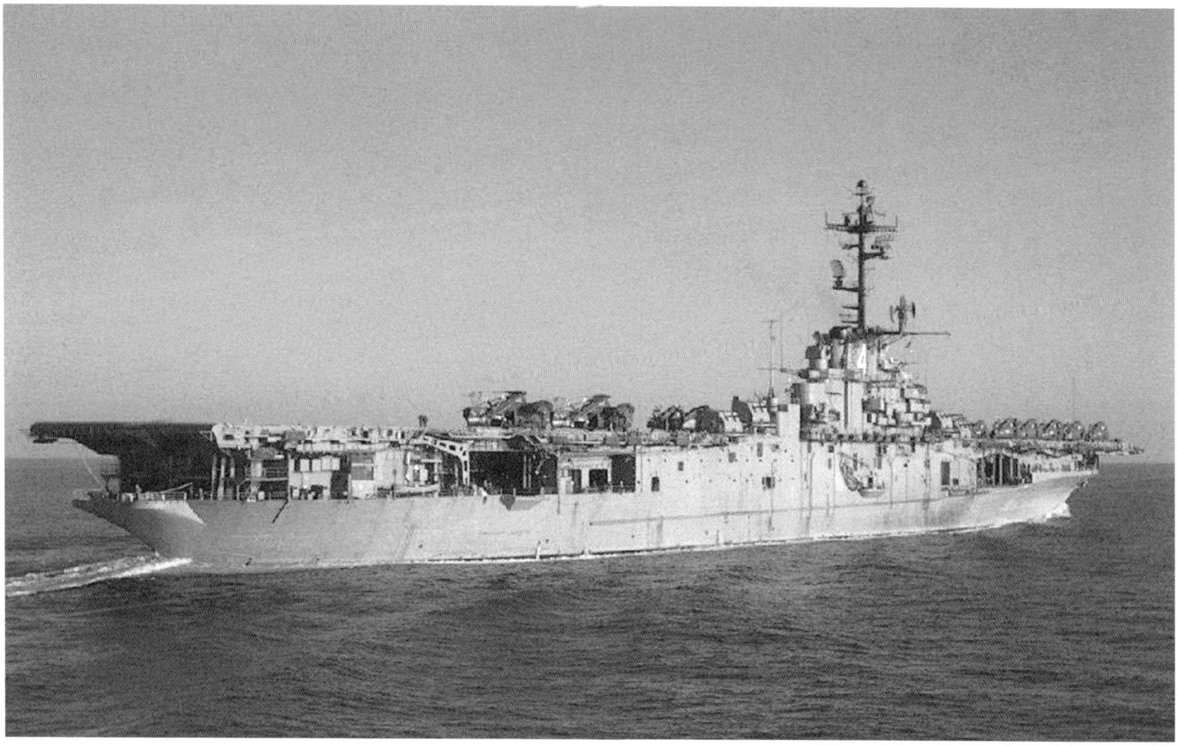

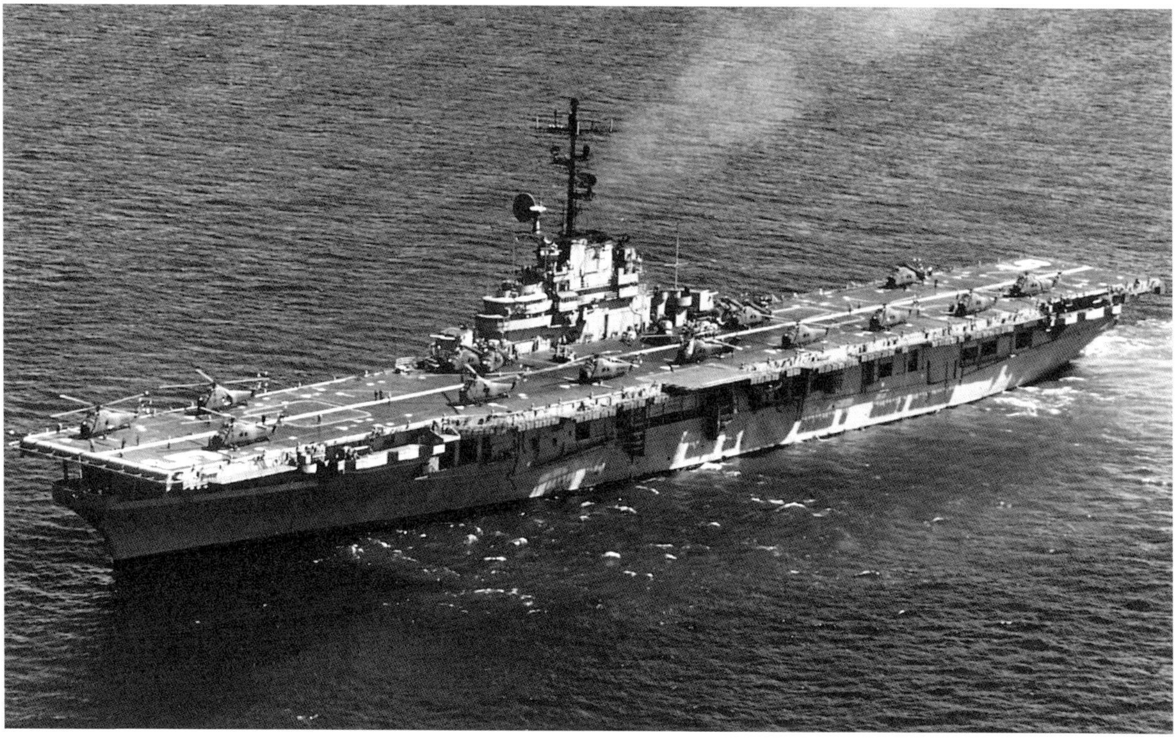

The third Essex class to be assigned to the amphibious assault role was USS *Valley Forge*, which was converted in 1961 and reclassified as LPH-8. She was on station when the Tonkin Gulf incident sparked US Navy involvement in the Vietnam War and subsequently she was almost continuously involved in missions to support US Marine units in assaults and fighting ashore before finally returning to Long Beach CA in October 1979. She was decommissioned the following January. During the Vietnam period the ship was awarded nine battle stars to add to the eight already earned in Korea. This photograph shows the ship in mid-1965 while transporting replacement A-4 Skyhawks and other stores to Okinawa as well as her embarked Marine helicopter air group. (NHHC)

Chapter Nine

Postscript

Originally conceived in the Second World War, the Essex class aircraft carriers played a significant role in the final defeat of Japan in 1945 and established the US as the world's premier seapower. They were subsequently called back into action in the Korean War and again to support US forces in Vietnam. Apart from *Franklin* (CV-13) and *Bunker Hill* (CV-17), both of which were decommissioned in 1947 (although not scrapped for another two decades), the majority of the class continued to serve in various capacities until the late 1960s; those that were involved in Vietnam deployments generally survived until the mid-1970s. One exception was the USS *Lexington* which served as training carrier until 1991 before being retired after a distinguished career lasting forty-eight years. She was subsequently preserved as a museum ship, as were three more Essex class – *Yorktown*, *Intrepid* and *Hornet*. Fittingly, all four of the preserved vessels saw arduous service in the Pacific during the Second World War and are therefore excellent representatives of a famous class of fighting ship.

Essex Class Aircraft Carriers – Fates

Essex (CV-9)	Decommissioned 30 July 1969. Stricken July 1973. Scrapped 1975.
Yorktown (CV-10)	Decommissioned 27 June 1970. Museum ship, Charleston SC, since 1975.
Intrepid (CV-11)	Decommissioned 15 March 1974. Museum ship, New York, since 1982.
Hornet (CV-12)	Decommissioned 25 June 1970. Stricken July 1989. Museum ship, Oakland CA, since 1998.
Franklin (CV-13)	Decommissioned 17 February 1947. Stricken 1 October 1964. Scrapped July 1966.
Ticonderoga (CV-14)	Decommissioned 1 September 1973. Sold for scrapping September 1975.
Randolph (CV-15)	Decommissioned 13 February 1969. Stricken 1 June 1973. Sold for scrapping 1975.

Lexington (CV-16)	Decommissioned 8 November 1991. Museum ship, Corpus Christi TX since 1992.
Bunker Hill (CV-17)	Decommissioned 9 January 1947. Stricken November 1966. Scrapped 1973.
Wasp (CV-18)	Decommissioned 1 July 1972. Scrapped 1973.
Hancock (CV-19)	Decommissioned 30 January 1976. Stricken 31 January 1976. Sold for scrapping September 1976.
Bennington (CV-20)	Decommissioned 15 January 1970. Stricken 20 September 1989. Sold for scrapping in India 1994.
Boxer (CV-21)	Decommissioned and stricken 1 December 1969. Sold for scrapping 1971.
Bon Homme Richard (CV-31)	Decommissioned 20 July 1971. Sold for scrapping 1992.
Leyte (CV-32)	Decommissioned 15 May 1959. Sold for scrapping 1970.
Kearsarge (CV-33)	Decommissioned 13 February 1970. Sold for scrapping 1974.
Oriskany (CV-34)	Decommissioned 30 September 1976. Stricken 1989. Sold for scrapping 1995 but repossessed 1997. Transferred to State of Florida in 2004 and sunk as an artificial reef off Pensacola in May 2006.
Reprisal (CV-35)	Order cancelled 12 August 1945. Scrapped on slipway.
Antietam (CV-36)	In reserve January 1963. Decommissioned 1969. Stricken May 1973. Sold for scrapping February 1974.
Princeton (CV-37)	Decommissioned 30 January 1970. Sold for scrapping May 1971.
Shangri-La (CV-38)	Decommissioned 30 July 1971. Stricken 15 July 1982. Sold for scrapping in Taiwan 1988.
Lake Champlain (CV-39)	Decommissioned 2 May 1966. Stricken 1 December 1969. Sold for scrapping 1972.
Tarawa (CV-40)	Decommissioned 1 May 1960. Stricken 1 June 1967. Sold for scrapping 3 October 1968.
Valley Forge (CV-45)	Decommissioned and stricken 15 January 1970. Sold for scrapping October 1971.
Iwo Jima (CV-46)	Order cancelled 12 August 1945. Scrapped on slipway.
Philippine Sea (CV-47)	Decommissioned 28 December 1958. Stricken 1 December 1969. Sold for scrapping March 1971.

The hull of the old warhorse USS *Bunker Hill* (CV-17) being broken up at an Oregon shipyard in 1973–4. Although fully repaired after her wartime damage, the ship was never recommissioned and after years in reserve was stricken from the Navy List in 1966. However, she was utilised as a stationary test platform for new electronic systems until being sold off for scrapping in July 1973. (NARA)

Decommissioned in 1973, the USS *Ticonderoga* (CVA-14) was sold for scrapping in 1975 and is shown after arriving alongside at Tacoma WA, where she was broken up. (Wikipedia Commons)

Above: The last of the Essex class to be retired was the USS *Lexington*, which in 1962 was designated as the US Navy's training aircraft carrier based at Pensacola FL. She subsequently served continuously in that role until finally retired in 1991 being initially classified as CVS, then CVT (1969) and finally AVT (1978). She is shown here underway in the Gulf of Mexico in 1978, and it is evident that all armament has been removed and the ship is basically a platform for student Navy and Marine pilots to hone their skills. (NHHC)

Opposite above: TA-4J Skyhawks of Pensacola based Training Wing 3 (TW-3) carrying out training flights aboard the USS *Lexington* (CVT-16) in the Gulf of Mexico, c. 1980. The Skyhawk in the foreground is being prepared for a catapult launch (note the raised blast screen in front of the aircraft) while in the background another Skyhawk has just done a 'bolter' from the angled deck. No doubt the latter's instructor is urgently reminding his student pilot that the air brakes are still extended! (NHHC)

Opposite below: USS *Yorktown* (originally CV-10) decommissioned on 27 June 1970 and was laid up in reserve for three years before being stricken in 1973. In 1974 she was donated to the Patriot's Point Development Authority (Charleston SC) and was towed there from New Jersey in June 1975. The first of the Essex class to be so preserved, she subsequently opened as a museum ship and is currently the focal point of the Patriot's Point Naval and Maritime Museum which also includes other warships such as the destroyer USS *Laffey* (DD724). (Josue Becerra via Wikipedia Commons)

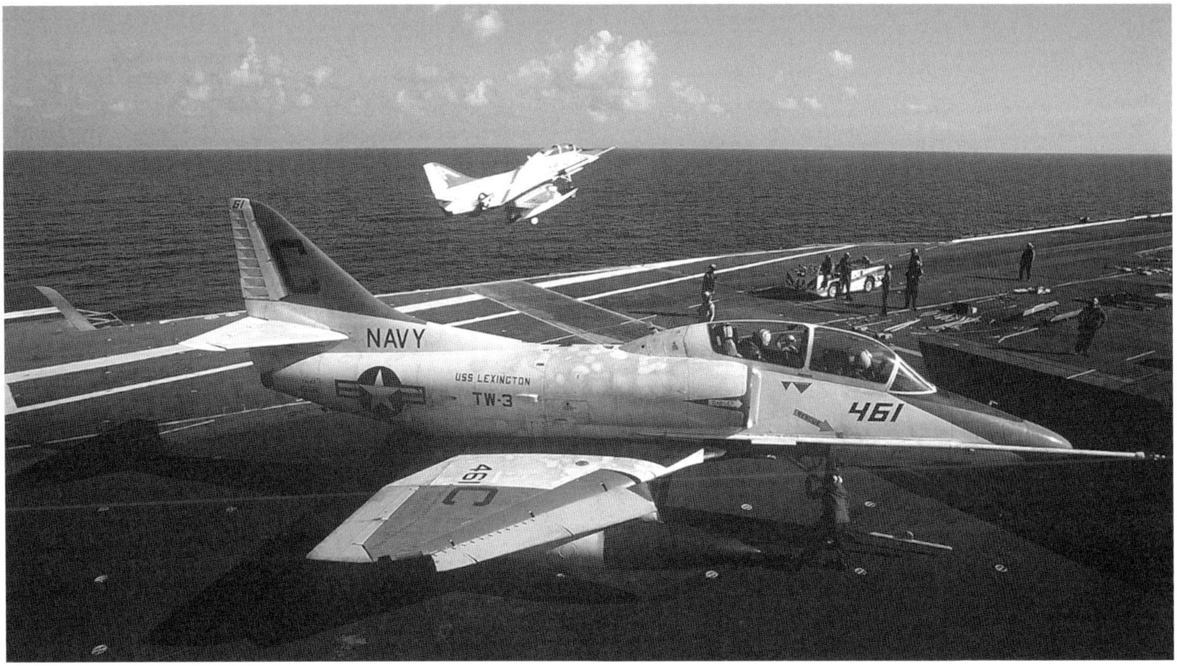
NAVY
USS LEXINGTON
TW-3
461

10

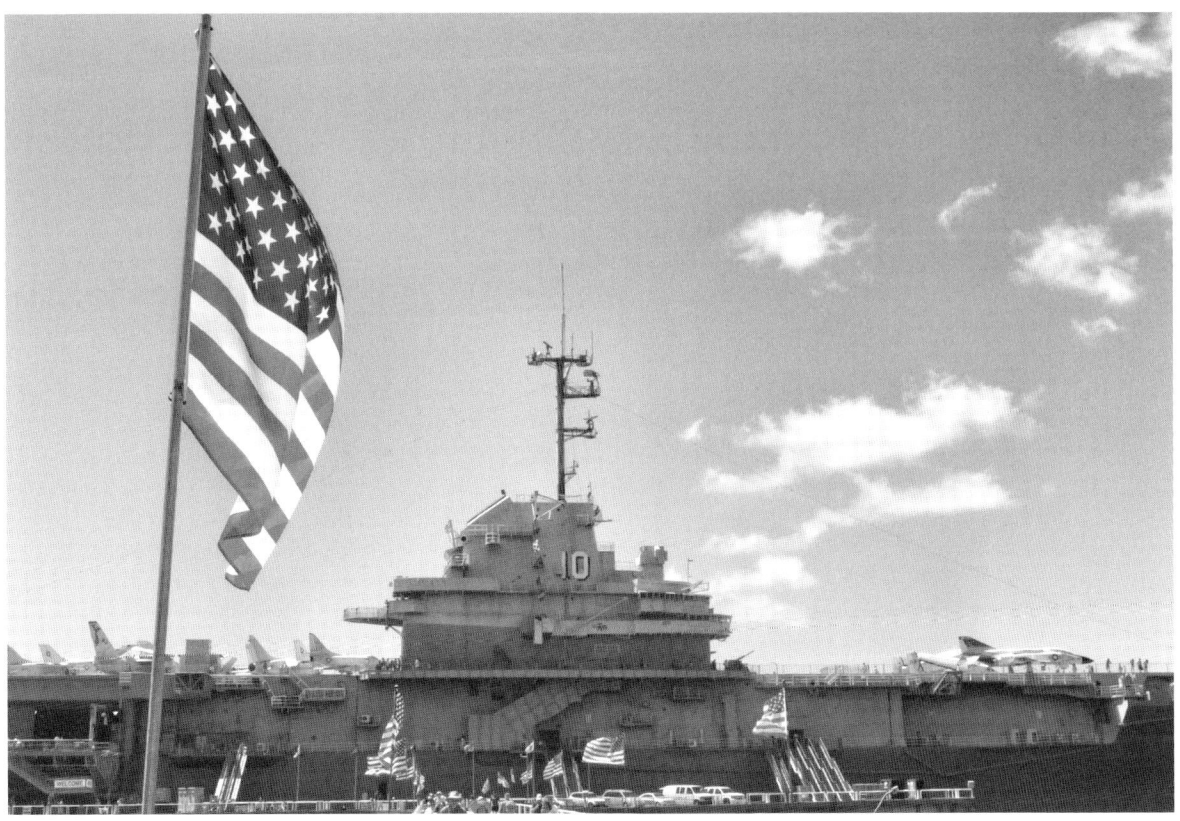

Above: The second Essex class carrier to be preserved as a museum ship was USS *Intrepid* (originally CV-11). Decommissioned in 1974, she was laid up and was scheduled for scrapping. However, a campaign to save this famous ship was successful and she was installed as the centrepiece of the Intrepid Sea-Air-Space Museum in 1982, based on Pier 86 on the New York west side waterfront. The ship underwent a major refurbishment in 2006–8, and in 2012 the Space Shuttle Enterprise was placed on display in a specially constructed pavilion alongside. (ASM)

Opposite above: Like the other preserved aircraft carriers, the *Intrepid*'s museum collection includes a variety of retired naval aircraft. A typical example is the USMC McDonnell F4-N Phantom II in the markings of VFMA-323. (ASM)

Opposite below: Although decommissioned in 1970, the USS *Hornet* (originally CV-12) was not stricken from the Navy List until 1989, and even then her fate was uncertain until she was designated as a National Historic Landmark in 1991 and later was donated to the Aircraft Carrier Hornet Foundation in 1998. She subsequently opened as a museum ship on 17 October 1998, moored at Alameda CA, which had been her home port for much of her eventful career. Currently open to public view, she has an interesting selection of naval aircraft including a Second World War FM-2 Wildcat and a Grumman F11F-1 Tiger. (Stan Shebs via Wikipedia Commons)

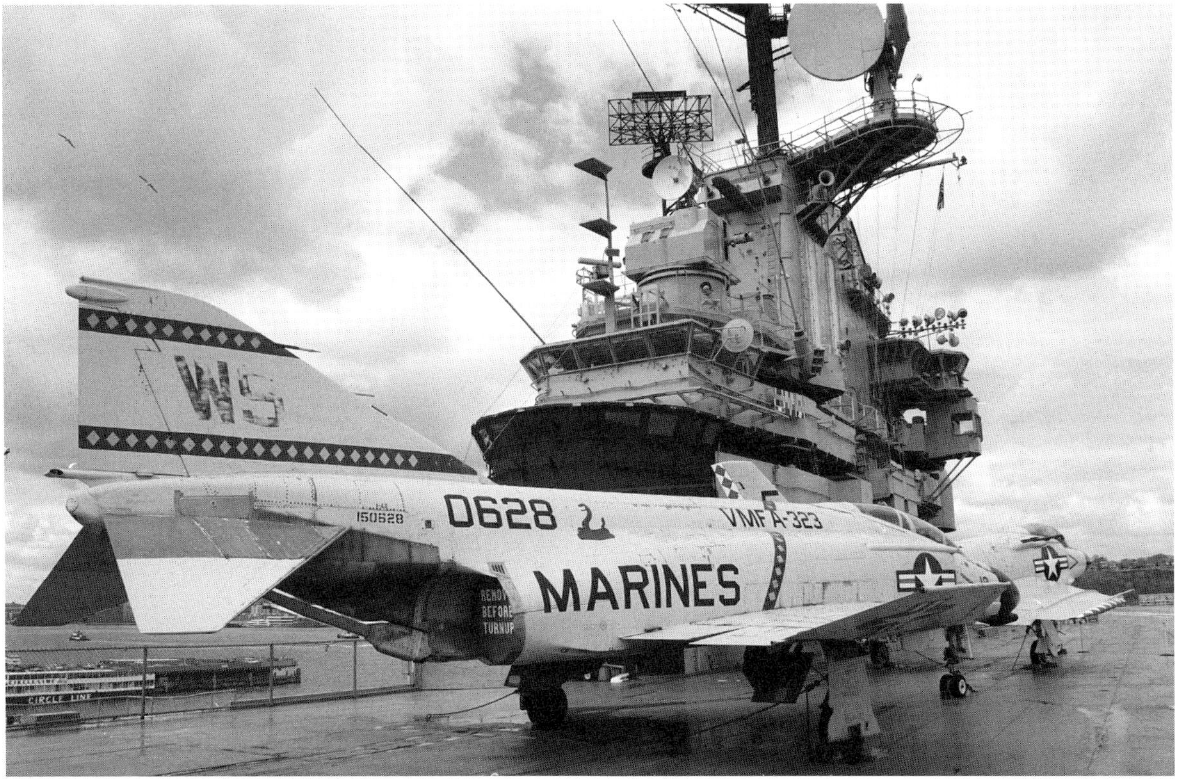
WS
0628
150628
VMFA-323
MARINES

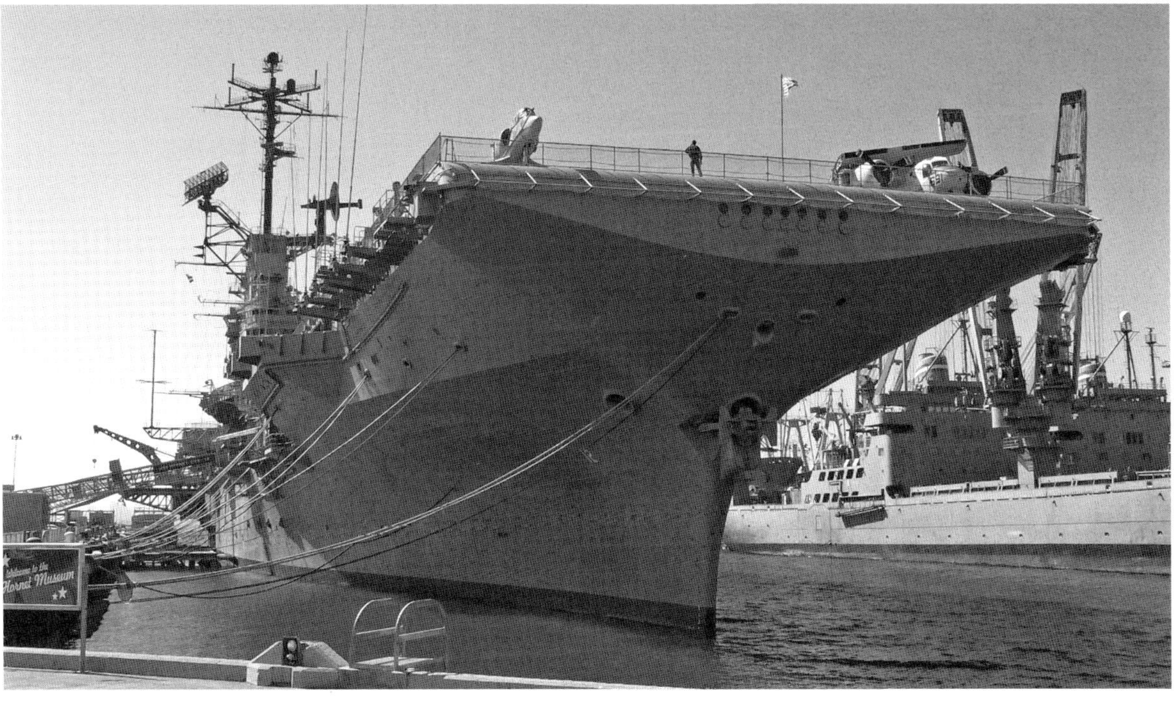

After a career spanning almost fifty years, the USS Lexington was finally decommissioned in 1991 and was laid up at Corpus Christi TX, where she opened to the public as a museum ship in 1992. Since then whole sections of the ship have been refurbished and made accessible to visitors as she provides a permanent memorial to the sailors and airmen for whom the ship was an important part of their naval careers. As this evening view shows, the ship is maintained in excellent condition and looks almost ready to put to sea again. (USS Lexington Museum via Robert Kymes)

Photo Credits

The following abbreviations at the end of each caption indicate the source and/or copyright of the relevant image:

ASM   Air Sea Media (author's copyright)
NARA   US National Archive and Record Agency (Still Image collection, College Park MD)
NASA   US National Aeronautics and Space Administration
NHHC   US Navy History and Heritage Command
NMNA   US Navy National Museum of Naval Aviation, Pensacola FL

Bibliography

Brown, J.D. (ed. David Hobbs), *Carrier Operations in World War II*, Seaforth Publishing, 2009.
Chesnau, Roger, *Aircraft Carriers of the World, 1914 to the Present. An Illustrated Encyclopedia*, Arms and Armour Press, 1984.
Francillon, René J., *Tonkin Gulf Yacht Club*, Conway Maritime Press, 1988.
Hallion, Richard P., *The Naval Air War in Korea*, Nautical & Aviation Publishing Company of America, 1986.
Johnson, E.R., *United States Naval Aviation 1919–1941*, McFarland & Co., 2011.
Lenton, H.T., *American Battleships, Carriers and Cruisers*, Macdonald & Co., 1968.
Morison, Samuel Eliot, *The Two-Ocean War*, Galahad Books, 1997.
Rohwr, J. and Hummelchen, G., *Chronology of the War at Sea 1939–1945*, Greenhill Books, 1992.
Swanborough, Gordon and Bowers, Peter M., *United States Navy Aircraft since 1911*, 2nd edn, Putnam, 1976
Terzibaschitsch, Stefan, *Aircraft Carriers of the US Navy*, Conway Maritime Press, 1980.
Thomas, Geoff, *US Navy Carrier Aircraft Colours*, Air Research Publications, 1989.